Contending with American Exceptionalism

Kori Schake

Contending with
American Exceptionalism

Kori Schake

IISS The International Institute for Strategic Studies

THE ADELPHI SERIES

The International Institute for Strategic Studies
Arundel House | 6 Temple Place | London | WC2R 2PG | UK

FIRST PUBLISHED March 2026 by **Routledge**
4 Park Square, Milton Park, Abingdon, Oxon, OX14 4RN

Simultaneously published in the USA and Canada by **Routledge**
605 Third Avenue, New York, NY 10158

Routledge is an imprint of the Taylor & Francis Group, an informa business

© The International Institute for Strategic Studies 2026

DIRECTOR-GENERAL AND CHIEF EXECUTIVE **Dr Bastian Giegerich**
SERIES EDITOR **Dr Benjamin Rhode**
ASSOCIATE EDITOR **Alice Aveson**
EDITORIAL **Rose Bell, Christopher Harder, Jill Lally, Michael Marsden**
DESIGN AND PRODUCTION **Alessandra Beluffi, Ravi Gopar, Jade Panganiban, James Parker, Kelly Verity-Cailes**
COVER ARTWORK **Amended version of Henry 'Hy' Mayer, *The Awakening*, 1915. PJ Mode Collection of Persuasive Cartography, Cornell University Library. Courtesy of Cornell University Library.**

The International Institute for Strategic Studies is an independent centre for research, information and debate on the problems of conflict, however caused, that have, or potentially have, an important military content. The Council and Staff of the Institute are international and its membership is drawn from almost 100 countries. The Institute is independent and it alone decides what activities to conduct. It owes no allegiance to any government, any group of governments or any political or other organisation. The IISS stresses rigorous research with a forward-looking policy orientation and places particular emphasis on bringing new perspectives to the strategic debate. Inclusion of a territory, country or state – or terminology or boundaries used in graphics or mapping – in this publication does not imply legal recognition or indicate support for any government or administration.

The Institute's publications are designed to meet the needs of a wider audience than its own membership and are available on subscription, by mail order and in good bookshops. Further details at www.iiss.org.

British Library Cataloguing in Publication Data
A catalogue record for this book is available from the British Library

Library of Congress Cataloging in Publication Data
A catalog record for this book has been requested

ADELPHI AP520-521: ISBN 978-1-041-33280-0 (paperback) / 978-1-003-78698-6 (eBook)
ADELPHI SERIES: ISSN 1944-5571 (print) / 1944-558X (online)

Contents

AUTHOR

Kori Schake leads the Foreign and Defense Policy team at the American Enterprise Institute (AEI) and holds the 2025–26 Kissinger Chair at the Library of Congress John W. Kluge Center. She is the author of *The State and the Soldier: A History of Civil–Military Relations in the United States* (Polity, 2025) and a number of other books. Before joining the AEI, Dr Schake was the Deputy Director-General of the International Institute for Strategic Studies (IISS). She has taught at Stanford University, the US Military Academy, Johns Hopkins University School of Advanced International Studies and the University of Maryland. She has had a distinguished career in government, working at the US Department of State, the US Department of Defense and the National Security Council at the White House. Dr Schake has a PhD and MA in government and politics from the University of Maryland, as well as an MPM from the University of Maryland School of Public Policy. Her BA in international relations is from Stanford University.

ACKNOWLEDGEMENTS

I am incredibly grateful to Robert Doar, the President of the American Enterprise Institute (AEI), for preserving it as a place of intellectual integrity, and for appreciating the need to shield time for thinking and writing amid the demands of management. I'm also deeply grateful to the fellows and research assistants of the AEI's Foreign and Defense Policy team for not mutinying while I am engaged in that thinking and writing. They continue to undertake challenging and consequential work with or without me.

Contending with American Exceptionalism

Introduction: The 'barbaric yawp'

It is a difficult time to be an American, to experience the fractiousness of a country narrowly divided politically and viciously contesting fundamental elements of our political, economic and social compact. It is also a difficult time to be a friend of America, especially one that has relied on international agreements and arrangements that are mutually beneficial, built on the foundation of American commitment. This is because to many Americans and foreign observers the Trump administration – and the majority of the American electorate that elected President Donald Trump and the Congress that is ratifying his appointments and permitting his policies – seems intent on destroying so much of what has made the United States successful, both domestically and internationally.

At the time of writing in 2025, the outcome of these policies cannot be predicted with certainty. Is it possible, as their proponents might argue, that these wrenching changes will amount to a 'rough wooing' that resets the wellsprings of American power, removing accrued constraints and unleashing vitality? Could it be that the threats and damage the Trump administration is doing to America and its role in the world will produce a domestic backlash that restores and reinforces the norms and policies that have made the US successful? Or is a 'hegemonic suicide' under way, as the US hurtles from being an economy that was the envy of the world and the leader of a secure and cost-effective international order to becoming a corrupt and lawless autocracy that aligns with other powerful predators?[1]

At the core of the issue is whether the United States is different enough from other countries to sustain this self-destructive damage and resurrect itself. A survey of the historical record of the decline of other hegemonic powers strongly suggests that it is not. The laws of gravity, physical and political, continue to operate and dictate outcomes. If one were forced to predict now, the hegemonic-suicide outcome appears the safest bet; even if American power can withstand the Trump era, the harm the United States is inflicting on itself and its allies will take a generation to repair, and we will be lucky to get through this period without an international economic collapse or a world war.

But while proponents of Trump's policies fatally misunderstand the factors that truly made America great, the advantages that created the United States and that the United States has created for itself are indeed distinctive, and may yet protect American prosperity and international dominance from those currently engaged in the vandalism of these factors. If so, this should serve not as a vindication of these policies but as their refutation.

Determining whether the United States can survive the current threats it is creating for itself and the international order it has fostered requires separating politicians' bloviating about American exceptionalism from a clear analysis of the elements that distinguish US society from other free and prosperous countries. Because there are indeed American distinctions; the question is whether those distinctions constitute enough difference to predicate an outcome that would be a historical outlier. Or, to put it more directly, how much difference will Trump make in the trajectory of American power?

While readers from other nations may feel similarly, we Americans have always considered ourselves exceptional. We are the people searching for the promised land. We are the people who rebel. We are the people who hold these truths to be self-evident. We are the people who will create a different kind of country and then a different kind of world order. We are the people exasperated with that beneficial order and willing to tear it down. We are a nation of immigrants arguing incessantly about immigration. We are a people both more litigious and more risk-tolerant than others.

American exceptionalism even comes through in sport: at home, Americans play sports they invent (American football, basketball and baseball) and hold 'world series' that include only American teams. Football (soccer), exported by England, has common rules everywhere it is played; not only do rules vary between the American and National leagues of baseball, but the dimensions of ballparks vary. Sport historian Jonathan Wilson captures American distinctiveness: 'They start to invent their own rules. They don't want to play by the world's rules ... There's something in the American psyche that says "we don't want a foreign game, we want our game".'[2]

At its most basic, American exceptionalism is simply the belief that the US is distinctive. But that simple idea carries enormous cultural and political freight in the American body politic. In the words of Donald E. Pease, it

> has provided US citizens with a representative form of self-recognition across the centuries. ... The founders imagined the United States as an unprecedentedly free, new nation based on founding documents – the

Declaration of Independence and the Constitution – that announced its unique destiny to become the champion of the universal rights of all humankind.[3]

More than just unique or distinctive, the concept of exceptionalism in American discourse means exemplary – worthy of emulation – and entails a dedication to making what is distinctive about the US universal.

Since its founding, John Winthrop's 1630 vision of the country as a 'shining city upon a hill' has influenced American self-conception, however often its policies and behaviours fail to accord.[4] Colin Powell pridefully claimed the US was unique in that it had repeatedly put its young soldiers at risk abroad and 'asked for nothing except enough ground to bury them in' (a perspective not shared by Mexico or the Philippines, among others).[5] President Barack Obama's comment that every nation considers itself exceptional set off a political firestorm.[6] And although he continued to give a very liberal definition of American exceptionalism to which he pretty clearly subscribed and ended with a lengthy discourse on ways in which the United States has been a unique force for progress and decency, it was politically damaging. Senator John McCain exemplified the belief in American exceptionalism, insisting: 'I refuse to accept that our values are morally equivalent to those of our adversaries'.[7] That the concept is such a valuable political cudgel is itself indicative. Most other countries, especially successful countries, do not have that debate as a feature of their political landscape.

President Trump, engenderer and avatar of much of the current concern, seems profoundly uninterested in the topic even as he attempts to wrench both the country in novel ways and the international order in directions that unilaterally advantage the US. He claims to be 'making America great again' while destroying the distinctiveness that has made it successful.

Trump's beliefs in the supremacy of material factors and power alone are misguided. The US is not exceptional merely because of its behemoth population and land mass replete with natural resources or the raucous capitalism that generates enormous wealth. It is exceptional because of its political creed and the remarkable flourishing that creed has produced. Moreover, the idea of America as different from and better than other countries is seminal to its role in the world. From that conception develops the vocation to shape the world in America's image.

The debate is consequential because during the time of its dominance first in the West and subsequently in the entirety of the international order, the US has genuinely been a different kind of hegemon than its predecessors. It created an 'empire by invitation', in which states were incentivised to participate by agreed rules to gain the benefits of economic prosperity and security, underwritten by the power of the American economy, its military and its culture.[8] This required enormous effort by the United States, often given hesitantly and stingily and even unreliably. But it also brought enormous gains in security and prosperity, both to the US and to the countries that opted in to the system. No dominant power has ever had as much voluntary assistance in upholding its dominance as has had the United States after the Second World War. Because the order is mutually beneficial, other countries have not organised against US power but have contributed to it – not as much and not as often as the US wants, but significantly – creating an economy of scale far in excess of what American power alone could amass.

One way to measure American exceptionalism is by counterfactual: if another state had access to US levels of power in the twentieth and twenty-first centuries, would it have behaved differently? The question answers itself. The reality, of course, is that no state has been able to generate comparable levels of power, which is in itself one indicator of US exceptionalism. But nor has any state historically been able to prevent hedging against its power by constructing an order acceptable to other powerful states, which is the other indicator of US exceptionalism. It voluntarily restrained the exercise of its own power, which previous hegemons did not. Whether either or both of those factors can be sustained under current conditions is at issue.

While the US gets many things wrong, what it gets right is very difficult to get right. So difficult, in fact, that no other state approaches the combination it achieves. And so difficult that the US is itself subject to loud disputes, exasperating contradictions, frequent setbacks and constant struggle. Walt Whitman, the first characteristically American poet, wrote in 'Song of Myself' an encapsulation of the country's spirit:

> I too am not a bit tamed, I too am untranslatable,
> I sound my barbaric yawp over the roofs of the world.[9]

American culture is shaped most prominently by immigration that creates both diversity and risk tolerance. Those attributes have resulted in a geographic expanse with vast resource reserves, decentralised power structures and a political system tied tightly to public attitudes. This system does not always produce good policy, but it does produce representative policy. And for the past 80 years, that policy has more often than not, and more often than was the case for previous hegemonic powers, been advantageous to itself and to other countries that opt into the American-led order.

The United States has never been comfortably internationalist, as the debate about exceptionalism reveals. Nor has it been notably cognisant of the extent to which its power relies on the concurrence and the active support of other countries. But it has now elected for a second time a president who thrashes against the voluntary restraints to which American governments have acceded in order to make US power more acceptable to those supporting states, which could result in the collapse of American power or attempts to create an international order that circumvents American influence.

Still, there are reasons to believe the wellsprings of power unique to the United States – beyond the material advantages the US enjoys – will remain and even become more dominant relative to other states. Because what is right about America may yet be the solution to what is currently dangerously wrong about America.[10] This book explores those wellsprings.

I. Foundation: the culture

Three things are essential in understanding the United States: firstly, that it is a country so innovative that in the midst of a global pandemic it could produce not just one but three life-saving vaccines; secondly, that it is a country so wealthy that it could not only provide those vaccines for free to its own population of 332 million but also make millions of doses available internationally; but finally, that it is a country in which a full third of the population would refuse a free, life-saving vaccine.[11]

Peter Drucker's famous conclusion that 'culture eats strategy for breakfast' holds for history and politics as well as business: nations have conceptions of themselves that condition their responses to events and shape their choices.[12] This the so-called 'realists' in international-relations theory fail to comprehend. Realists purport that every state reacts identically, and is driven to maximise its power. But it is simply untrue that post-1945 Germany's conception of itself is the same as that of pre-1945 Germany; it was not just forced to change, it wanted to be different. Nor is it true that America's conception of itself drove it to maximise its power when it became dominant: it voluntarily limited its power and embedded it in international institutions to reduce resistance and increase legitimacy.

As Frederick Jackson Turner propounded in 'The Significance of the Frontier in American History' (1893), 'behind institutions, behind constitutional forms and modifications lie the vital forces that call these organs into life and shape them to meet changing conditions'.[13] While Turner's frontier thesis falters in its most expansive claims about all aspects of American culture being dictated by the opportunities and dangers of an expanding frontier, he was unquestionably right that culture underlies and shapes political structures, economic practices and conceptions of violence.

America's overriding sense of itself as exceptional stems from the nation's founding in revolution. We are the people who rebel. Historian David Kennedy described Americans as 'rebellious by nature, rootless by circumstance, and ravenous to possess the vast territories that beckoned to their westward'.[14] Historian Bertha Ann Reuter captured the same sentiment, considering Americans 'people too radical either in religion or politics or both to live peaceably in their original home'.[15]

The differential in risk tolerance with other prosperous free societies is the most striking characteristic of American culture. Its taproot is to be found in immigration: nearly all Americans are immigrants, voluntarily or forcibly (as in the case of slaves or Native Americans).[16] Choosing to immigrate is strongly suggestive of necessity – of having little to lose by leaving, and the belief that a better future could be crafted elsewhere. Societal practices and government policies in the US reinforce the belief that most immigrants can be safely in the middle class in the course of a single generation.[17]

Immigration brings a diversity that forces Americans to confront our bigotry and unfairness. Governing over diversity is incredibly hard, and Americans confront it every day. The ringing clarity of the truths held to be self-evident also very often runs up against either local or general opposition. One illustrative example is the issue of whether to provide bilingual education: should school lessons in particular districts such as Los Angeles be offered in Spanish if a sizeable minority of students are native Spanish speakers? Would doing so trap Spanish speakers into lower-income jobs by denying them English proficiency? Would it be fair to the other children in the Los Angeles school district who between them speak more than 100 different languages?[18] Would it result in higher dropout rates, and therefore greater economic and social costs? What decision rules should govern such a question? American history is the story of extending rights from a privileged group to those excluded from their protection or advantage, and then dealing with the social and political complications of resentment.

When Americans initially set out to define themselves, they did so in contrast to their closest approximation, which was Britain. They shifted their frame of self-reference from subjects to citizens. The great historian of America's early modern period, Gordon Wood, concludes that by 1815, 'the cultural focus of this huge expansive nation was no longer abroad but was instead directed at its own boundless possibilities'.[19]

American culture signifies the democratisation of everything: politics, religion, language, even fashion. It is characterised by a veneration of progress, in all its vulgarity and unruliness. It is, and at least since 1815 has been, self-absorbed, convinced always of its own exceptionalism. Unique at the time in passing governance from an enlightened elite to the masses (what Thomas Jefferson exalted as 'the boisterous sea of liberty'), Americans demonstrated a risk tolerance, even among political conservatives, that stood out and continues to shape their society.[20]

Even for the founding generation, American politics often produced disappointing results. Every single founding father worried the country was failing, that democracy had run its course.[21] It took 36 rounds of voting in 1800 to elect the talents of Jefferson (whom one might have considered a qualified candidate) to the presidency, those men now cast in marble slandering each other pseudonymously in the newspapers. As Alexander Hamilton wrote in 'The Federalist No. 1', 'happy will it be if our choice should be directed by a judicious estimate of our true interests, unperplexed and unbiassed by considerations not connected with the public good. But this is a thing more ardently to be wished, than seriously to be expected.'[22]

Exceptionalism in the founding era compounded in the nineteenth century with westward expansion after the American Civil War. As I wrote a decade ago, the frontier engendered the defining mythology of American culture:

> Gained was a country of continental expanse, social and economic mobility, breathtaking tolerance for turbulence and risk, wealth creation on a scale not previously imagined, an abiding belief in the necessity and righteousness of armed force, ennoblement of the individual crafting his or her own fate in a harsh wilderness, urbanization of the industrial revolution balanced by rural landowners, and the genius of the founders' political structures accommodating both in the respective houses of Congress.[23]

Entrepreneurialism – what Alexander Hamilton described as 'financial esprit' – was always integral to American culture. Gordon Wood assesses that 'nowhere in the Western world was business and working for profit more honoured'.[24] Britain being the closest cultural and political comparison of the time

shows just how much more the ethos of entrepreneurialism marks American culture. Even British political reformers
recoiled at the greedy, grasping nature of American material-
ism: poet and cultural critic Matthew Arnold's *Discourses in
America* are replete with condescension and concern:

> in a democratic community like this, with its newness,
> its magnitude, its strength, its life of business, its sheer
> freedom and equality, the danger is in the absence of
> the discipline of respect; in hardness and materialism,
> exaggeration and boastfulness; in a false smartness, a
> false audacity, a want of soul and delicacy.[25]

Nor were foreign critics wrong about the excesses of
American culture. Frederick Jackson Turner cautioned in 1893
that 'individualism in America has allowed a laxity in regard
to governmental affairs which has rendered possible the spoils
system and all the manifest evils that follow from the lack of a
highly developed civic spirit'.[26]

Contemporary American attitudes to gun violence reveal
most baldly the cultural chasm between the US and other free
societies: Americans tolerate astonishingly high rates of gun
deaths without generating the political consensus to meaning-
fully restrict gun possession. In 2023, there were 47,000 deaths
in the US from gun-related injuries.[27] As the satirical newspaper
The Onion routinely headlines, '"No Way to Prevent This", Says
Only Nation Where This Regularly Happens'.[28] This would not
be tolerated anywhere else, and as such it serves to measure the
distance of American culture from others, even those similarly
constituted by politics, religion, immigration and ethnic origin.

France, also a nation of people who rebel and who proclaim
universalist aims, provides a useful contrast to the US. Culturally,
the French love themselves in grandeur – in high art and mass

demonstrations of protest, in political and legal concepts dictated from on high, and in laws restricting working hours – whereas Americans love themselves in the accessibility of culture, the democratisation of everything, of localised solutions, common law, dedication to working relentlessly and variable rules.

The French newspaper *La Liberté* maligned the United States in 1932, writing in fury that 'Americans are the only race which passed directly from barbarism to decadence without knowing civilization'.[29] This accusation has been variously attributed over the years, and resonates not only for its humour and stereotypical European condescension of the US; it also captures the shibboleth-destroying nature of American culture. As former US poet laureate Robert Pinsky has written, 'American culture as I have experienced it seems so much in process, so brilliantly and sometimes brutally in motion, that standard models for it fail to apply'.[30]

Culture in most countries is an elite affair, resulting from success and patronage of the moneyed classes, whereas America produced the blues out of the misery of its slave-owning legacy, jazz from fearless improvisation by the excluded and rap from its urban despair. American culture is fuelled as much by its social failures as by its successes. Jazz, in particular, is profoundly American, being expertly described: 'in contrast to harmonious, complex, exclusive Culture, jazz was denounced as discordant, uncivilized, overly accessible, and subversive to reason and order'.[31] So it is with hip hop now; it is a musical culture concordant with the political and economic culture of its generative society, and the diversity of that society drives accessibility that then makes international adoption more likely.

France loves itself in the exclusivity and perfection of high culture; America loves itself in the democratisation of culture. France may have the exquisite artistry of Versailles and the world's most beautiful and opulent opera house, but America has both Disneyland and architect Frank Gehry's Walt Disney

Concert Hall, with its perfect acoustics and sleek steel reflecting the cerulean expanse of southern California skies. America's gift to high fashion is leisurewear, creating cultural cachet for wearing sneakers with suits.

France provided an earlier *lingua franca*, but American English has become the international language of both commerce and culture. British users fume that some computer dictionaries allow selection of British English while 'English' connotes the American variant, with its un-anglicised spellings and frequent inventions. As the American novelist (and immigrant from the USSR) Gary Shteyngart observes, no country other than the US 'has the capacity to impose its worldview on the rest of the globe with such stubborn resilience'.[32]

Nowhere is American culture more pronounced than at the movies, a genre invented elsewhere and made American by émigrés. In a perfect illustration requiring knowledge of riparian geography of the American Midwest to decipher, Vivian C. Sobchack writes:

> Exploring the connections between American studies and film studies is rather like standing before the confluence of the Mississippi and Ohio Rivers. The observer is confronted with the necessity of stepping into two rivers at once or not getting wet at all. Film Studies is as integral a part of American Studies as American Studies is a part of Film Studies; the separate currents are so commingled at their meeting point that the waters can no longer be clearly distinguished.[33]

At the movies and far beyond, American culture is a function of the profound fact that the United States is an immigrant society. While assimilation is the narrative of American culture, that has seldom actually reflected its lived experience. America is less a melting pot than a mosaic.[34] But the rivers of ethnicity converge on agreed elements of 'Americanness', always contested and shifting in composition, but anchored in the founding principles. And 'the presence of large numbers of talented immigrants in Hollywood, academia and the high-tech industries has pushed American institutions to be more meritocratic and open to innovation than they would be otherwise'.[35]

There is a tendency, especially among catastrophists about contemporary America, to harken back to a time when the political establishment was composed of statesmen rather than grubby and often corrupt partisans, when Americans were supposedly enlightened internationalists rather than crazed conspiracists suspicious of global intrusions and hostile to foreign obligations. But that is chimerical, and gives Americans both more and less credit than we deserve: more, in that it presumes we were ever better than we are; and less, because it fails to appreciate how much effort goes into producing better outcomes than the solipsism of American culture would otherwise dictate.

To take one example, many Atlanticists yearn for the America of the Dwight D. Eisenhower administration (1953–61), when the president was decent and predictable and unflinching about the responsibilities of leading the free world. But recall that Eisenhower had to be cajoled into the race for the Republican presidential nomination to prevent Robert Taft from winning, which would have signalled the end of NATO and the ramping up of tariffs. And Eisenhower not only sanctioned attacks on President Harry Truman and Eisenhower's own mentor George Marshall, he also declined to rein in Joseph McCarthy's attacks on American diplomats and defence professionals. Moreover, he had to federalise the entire Arkansas National Guard and send the 101st Airborne Division to enforce a Supreme Court decision and protect black students attempting to attend integrated schools. And president Eisenhower forcibly deported more than a million people, including American citizens, during *Operation Wetback* in 1954.[36] He lied to the American people about U-2 overflights of the Soviet Union. That most Atlanticist president advocated deployment of US troops to Europe only until allies restored their economies and could defend themselves, had his secretary of state threaten in 1954 an 'agonizing reappraisal' of American commitment to Europe's defence, and moved to bankrupt Britain during the 1956 Suez Crisis. American culture has never been as comfortably liberal as our advocates would hope it to be.

American culture is, at least, self-satirising. Perhaps no one captures it as well as novelist Philip Roth:

> the American writer in the middle of the 20th century has his hands full in trying to understand, and then describe, and then make credible much of the American reality. It stupefies, it sickens, it infuriates, and finally it is even a kind of embarrassment to one's own meager imagination. The actuality is continually outdoing our talents, and the culture tosses up figures almost daily that are the envy of any novelist.[37]

II. Infrastructure: the politics

It is important to remember that the American government was formed by people who distrusted government. Coming out of the liberal governance traditions of the Netherlands and Great Britain, American colonists nonetheless were convinced that they suffered abject tyranny – at least enough of them were convinced to foment rebellion.[38] Skating past the noble sentiments in its preamble, the Declaration of Independence is an intemperate condemnation of 27 governmental impositions on local autonomy.

Getting from colonies to states to a union was, as so much of history, chancy. Luring colonies with different ethnicities, economies, religions and civic traditions required balances of power sufficiently protective of differences to gain consent, so representation in the House benefitted populous states while the Senate prevented the less populous being overwhelmed, and governance power was distributed not only between the branches of federal government but also between federal and state governments. Even that diffusion of authority required assurance in the Second Amendment that states would retain the resort to arms against the federal government to garner assent for the Constitution to be ratified.

The American Constitution has been described as 'an invitation to struggle' because, as 'The Federalist No. 51' attests, 'its several constituent parts may, by their mutual relations, be the means of keeping each other in their proper places. ... Ambition must be made to counteract ambition.'[39] Alexis de Tocqueville captures the genius of the system: 'in the United States the majority, which so frequently displays the tastes and the propensities of a despot, is still destitute of the more perfect instruments of tyranny'.[40] As James Madison writes in 'The Federalist No. 10', 'we behold a republican remedy for the diseases most incident to republican government'.[41]

Polybius writes of the Romans' constitution that 'its peculiar character contributed largely to their success'.[42] And granting that the United States has in times of previous crisis often been extraordinarily fortunate in its leadership, Polybius's conclusion is also true of the US. The US government is structured to govern over diversity. While many decry Washington gridlock, that is the American system working as intended, which is to say that the US government is designed to do nothing or to vacillate with transient policies until someone wins the political argument. The only way to gain enduring commitment is to enshrine domestic political agreement in legislation that passes constitutional adjudication by the courts, and the only way to garner enduring international obligation is to have the Senate consent to ratification and both houses to apportion funding.

To a greater extent than parliamentary systems of republican governance, the US system is tied tightly to public opinion. The office of the president is predominant in election calculations, defining the political choice more so than prime ministers do in parliamentary systems. The durability of two political parties, and the amorphousness of political beliefs that define and separate them, are likewise uncommon to other democracies. The two-party system results in elections where 'the people are a sovereign whose vocabulary is limited to "yes" or "no"'.[43] And elections for the House of Representatives are held every two years, giving the US no respite from electoral politics. These structural factors make politics in the US more pendular than in other free societies, frequently swinging back and forth as public attitudes change.

The American political system is more personalist than those of most other free societies. Molly Worthen writes that

> charisma is in no way a peculiarly American phenomenon. But it has a peculiarly interesting and influential history in America due to the country's religious and ethnic diversity and its exaggerated, messy version of the Reformation, a saga of supercharged individualism and meaning-making that is unique to the United States. The country became a proving ground for metaphysical entrepreneurs who sought both to soothe and galvanize humans' mixed feelings about

freedom and their desire for someone to grant them a
role in a story larger than themselves.[44]

Charisma suits a presidential system, wherein voters cast
their ballots for the standard bearer.

The United States is, by expanse and political design, a
provincial country. Its vast regions have distinctive accents
and even vocabularies, disparate economic drivers, specific
immigration patterns and ethnic compositions. States control
the terms of federal elections, establish independent education
and welfare policies, and even retain capable military forces
in the form of National Guard troops under the command
of governors. To speak of the 'national' is to aggregate from
the specificity of state authorities and demands. Abraham
Lincoln personified provincial political acumen, rising to
national prominence from the rough-hewn frontier to become
America's secular saint. Yet he held fast to the political realities
of the system, declaring in 1864, 'I hope to have God on my
side, but I must have Kentucky'.[45]

Distrust of government and westward expansion outpac-
ing governance reinforced the voluntary civic organisation
of which de Tocqueville writes so memorably. Because we
distrust our government, Americans find ways to solve problems outside the confines of governmental action to a greater
degree than other free societies. Both the risk tolerance and
the independence of state legal and regulatory structures
reinforce innovations like charter schools and variations
on welfare programmes. As Tim Carney writes, 'America is
the land of opportunity because America is the land of civil
society'.[46] It even holds true internationally: the US government is one of the stingiest providers of foreign aid, but
the United States is the most generous donor nation overall
because of the Gates Foundation, Rotary Clubs, religious

groups and the myriad other non-governmental organisations that seek to change the world.

A striking example of the power of American civil society and federalism is that in 2018, after the Trump administration had withdrawn the US from the Paris Agreement and reversed numerous environmental regulations, the US remained on track to meet its Paris climate commitments – because governors, mayors, business executives and American consumers continued to advance the goals of the agreement.[47] Another example is the way religious groups, prominently including the Catholic Church and its American pope, are working against Trump's recent surge of federal deportations.[48]

III. Conveyor: the economy

Whereas most other countries have political, cultural and economic power concentrated in their national capital, those elements are distributed across the geographic vastness of the United States: political power is vested in Washington DC (purposely separated by the founders from the financial capital); the country's financial centre is New York City; its technology hubs are Silicon Valley in California and Boston in Massachusetts; while Los Angeles (movies) and New York (theatre) vie for the title of cultural bastion. Perennial arguments debate whether the country's best pizza is in New York or Chicago, with Los Angeles and Detroit recent contenders.[49] There are 3,982 degree-granting colleges in the United States, 1,625 of them public institutions.[50] Sixteen American universities are currently ranked in the world's top 25, and they, too, bestride the whole country: Massachusetts, New Jersey, California, Connecticut, Illinois, Pennsylvania, Maryland, New York, Michigan and Washington state.[51]

Conquest of the North American continent, including territory taken from both neighbouring countries Mexico and Canada by force or flood of immigrants, provided the United States with a remarkable resource platform of arable land, water and energy. The US has the largest area of arable land of any country, with 390m acres.[52] US farming both feeds the US and is the world's leading exporter despite using only a fraction of the labour of other agricultural producers.[53] By dint of both natural endowment and technological innovation, the US has become the world's largest oil producer and the second-largest producer of energy overall.[54]

The American economy relies much less on trade than do other developed economies: only 11% of US GDP derives from trade in goods and even services, which are considered the country's great strength.[55] Research by Robert Keohane and Joseph S. Nye, Jr. demonstrates that US trade

> is extremely asymmetric with China, Mexico, and the Association of Southeast Asian Nations, all of which have an export–import ratio of more than two to one with the United States. For Japan (roughly 1.8 to 1), South Korea (1.4 to 1), and the European Union (1.6 to 1), those ratios are also asymmetric.[56]

These asymmetries give the US significant power in leveraging access to its behemoth market.

The US has the world's deepest and broadest capital markets, both public and venture capital. The US$65 trillion combined value of US stocks comprises half the global total, an increase from before the 2008 global financial crisis.[57] Whereas in 2015 the total volume of equity trading in Europe was roughly equal to the S&P 500, now US volumes are four times larger.[58] Venture capital is practically synonymous with American financial esprit, Sebastian Mallaby concluding that 'the venture capital approach of high-risk, high-reward experiments does represent a distinctive way of coming at the world'.[59] Private equity (otherwise known as venture capital) from the US financed US$208 billion within the US in 2024 and American businesses attracted US$74.6bn in foreign venture capital.[60]

The cultural risk tolerance of American society thrums through its economy. 'Chapter 11 bankruptcy' is emblematic of what makes the American economy more dynamic than other developed economies. Chapter 11 of the US Bankruptcy Code permits a business that cannot service its debts to file for protection from creditors in federal court. It allows the business to remain in control of its assets and to continue to operate while a judge supervises reorganisation to return it to solvency. The objective is to rehabilitate the business rather than favouring repayment of creditors. Chapter 11 is both part of how the US triggered the 2008 financial crisis and a major reason the US economy rebounded more quickly than others: US$3.5trn of corporate debt was judged distressed or in default and by 2009 US$1.8trn of public-company assets were under Chapter 11 protections.[61] Keeping businesses functioning, and thereby people employed, was also the argument that underwrote the American approach to financial support during the COVID-19 pandemic.

American risk tolerance is also evident in the technology sector. Whereas most developed economies regulate to prevent harm, the US system tends only to regulate when substantial harm has occurred. That makes US firms more experimental (and, of course, also increases harm). The US has 690 private tech companies valued at more than US$1bn, representing a combined value of US$2.53trn; by contrast, China has 162 and the European Union 107.[62] Theodore Roosevelt said 'when I am in California, I am not in the West. I am west of the West.'[63] The same holds true for the US compared to other developed economies and free societies: we are the west of the West, where the problems but also the advantages first accrue.

Social media is one of the most striking examples of the US as the west of the West: American firms invented it and demonstrated its advantages, drawing users into a global network of information, utilising predatory algorithms to addict and extract value from users, and then utilising that value for monetary or political gain, skewing and embittering public discourse and allowing anonymous users and foreign governments access to significant political effect.[64] Critics describe social-media platforms as 'technological wrecking balls responsible for shattering the norms and institutions that kept citizens tethered to a shared reality, creating an informational Wild West dominated by viral falsehoods, bias-confirming echo chambers, and know-nothing punditry'.[65] Elon Musk would be hobbled in any other country, but the US benefits from his remarkable inventiveness because it tolerates his destructive impulses. Other governments, seeing the potential to damage, regulate or control access: China refusing its citizens uncensored social-media access; the EU seeking to defang its harms. The US does neither, letting it burn on.

If artificial intelligence (AI) makes the economic future unrecognisable and causes anywhere near the social upheaval its architects are anticipating, the US is likely where that future will find its frontier. *The Economist* anticipates that 'politics would therefore be volatile. Governments would have to rethink everything from the tax base to education to the protection of civil rights.'[66] The US may not win the developmental sweepstakes, and it will surely not preventatively govern its uses, but as the most risk-tolerant free society – the west of the West – it will likely be where discovery of problems and development of solutions first occur.

Because 'radical rethinks tend to come from outsiders', immigration fuels innovation in the US economy.[67] More than 50m Americans are immigrants, comprising 15% of the total population of the country.[68] And 41% of those immigrants have a college education (the rate was even higher before the huge influx via illegal border crossings during the Biden administration).[69] Moreover, immigrants are around 80% more likely to found a company than US-born citizens, according to a Massachusetts Institute of Technology study.[70] Those companies tend to have more employees and be high-growth businesses, creating jobs rather than taking existing jobs.[71]

Abundance of labour, weak unions, more permissive labour laws (and willingness to work longer hours and take fewer holidays), less regulation, higher productivity for lower wages and a stingy social-welfare net give American-based businesses distinct advantages when compared to other developed economies.[72] Economist Michael Strain calculates that 'fewer than four out of every 100 workers who wants a job cannot find one'.[73] Furthermore, venture capital, market integration and stock options as compensation to give incentives make American businesses more agile. In the past half-century, the US created 241 companies with market capitalisation greater than US$10bn, Europe only 14; and the typical US company trading in the top ten was founded in 1985.[74] As an EU business leader reflects, 'what is different in America is the speed of almost everything'.[75] These advantages have produced a dynamic economy comprising roughly 25% of nominal global output with remarkable consistency across more than 60 years.[76]

Per capita GDP in the United States clocks in at US$85,800. By contrast, China's per capita GDP is US$13,300, or US$27,100 even when adjusted for price differences.[77] And whereas 20 years ago it appeared the Chinese economy might power through the middle-income trap and surpass the US economy, both government policies and demography now suggest China's growth rates may have subsided to barely higher than those of the US, making the wealth gap insurmountable.[78] Europe's economy, which was roughly the size of America's 15 years ago, is now one-third smaller.[79]

Political structures abet these economic advantages by insulating the Federal Reserve ('Fed' – the US central bank) from both executive and legislative control. Market reaction to President Trump's threats to fire Federal Reserve Chair Jerome Powell (something the president does not have legal authority to do) demonstrates just how much Fed independence advantages the US economy: if the president or Congress were able to manipulate interest rates, US investments would be much less attractive. The requirement for Federal Reserve debates to be made public (with a time lag), and for the Fed chair to justify forward-looking guidance and decisions to Congress, make the process more transparent and predictable, which also draws investment to the US and encourages use of the dollar internationally.

These advantages, both natural and constructed, created the basis for the US dollar to become the holding currency of global economic interaction. The dollar accounts for US$6.6trn in foreign-exchange transactions *daily*, 90% of the total, according to the Bank for International Settlements (BIS).[80] The BIS also calculates that the dollar is utilised in half of global trade, accounts for half of all international debt securities and cross-border loans, and supplies 60% of foreign-exchange reserves. Its centrality permits profligacy by the US government, keeping interest rates low and bond purchases attractive. Without dollar centrality, the eye-popping US$37trn in national debt and US$1.34trn deficit for 2025 would result in much steeper downgrades of US credit. As Moody's drily concludes of the

US fundamentals, 'these scores are a long way below the "a3" Fiscal Strength factor score consistent with an Aa1 rating'.[81]

The US Federal Reserve also serves as the liquidity provider of last resort, both domestically and internationally, through interbank loans ensuring dollar availability.[82] Economist Michael Pettis concludes 'the role of the US dollar in the global system of trade and capital flows is unprecedented, mainly because of the unprecedented role the US economy plays in global trade and capital imbalances': the US absorbs fully half of the global surplus in savings from both advanced and developing economies.[83] As a result, for the US, the capital account drives trade. Replacing the dollar would require another country to absorb current-account surpluses – signifying 'the end of the current global trading system'.[84]

IV. Enforcer: the military

The US military has only won one war out of the four it has fought since 1945, yet it remains globally dominant by virtually every metric of military power. Defence spending of US$967bn in 2024 makes the US budget by far the largest (although by Mackenzie Eaglen's calculations, China is now approaching US levels).[85] It is the only military that can conduct combat operations at scale reaching across thousands of miles. Measures of military equipment reveal 'the persistent dominance of the United States in terms of total, generally weighted stock of heavy and medium military equipment (exceeding one-quarter of the annual global total from the 1970s through 2015)'.[86] The US military pioneered the integration of combat arms across military services (known as 'jointness') that compounds proficiency and is enviously emulated by all other major militaries. It fights often, seasoning its leadership. It conducts warfare training so realistic that it incurs around 300 deaths per year in exercises.[87]

The American way of war relies fundamentally on logistics: American soldiers may not look like much marching in parades, but 'if you want a Burger King anywhere on the globe in 48 hours', they can get it done.[88] In 2018, US Transportation Command carried out 'more than 1,900 air missions during an average week and has 25 ships underway and 10,000 ground shipments operating in 75 percent of the world's countries'.[89] During the humiliating debacle of the US withdrawal from Afghanistan in 2021, the US military was flying 20 C-17 sorties from Afghanistan every 24 hours – while utilising less than 20% of its cargo fleet.[90] No other armed forces in the world could surge operations to such a level irrespective of timeline.

This the US military accomplishes with a force comprising only 0.5% of the US population – a force that has been recruited rather than conscripted since 1973. For 250 years, that American military has never been a threat to democracy, accepting civilian control and professionally carrying out policies it often advised against. And Americans love the military for that, routinely citing it as the institution in public life in which they have the greatest trust. Even when confidence in the US military was at its lowest point in two decades (2023), 60% of Americans had a great deal or quite a lot of confidence in their armed forces.[91] In keeping with the theme of risk tolerance, the US public is more willing to use its military than are most other countries, especially if that does not entail long-term efforts.

The value accorded to US military training and equipment is reflected in the number of countries that have security agreements with the US (more than 50), have US troops stationed voluntarily on their territory (more than 1,000 troops are stationed in each of ten countries; overall there are 243,000 US forces stationed overseas), are involved in US military training programmes (2.4m foreign military personnel trained between 1999 and 2016) or purchase US weapons systems (60 countries).[92]

No other country can project power globally in the way the US can. No other has equivalent intelligence collection and analysis and operations at their disposal, or the command and control, or the lift and logistics. According to IISS research, replicating just the US military and intelligence contribution to European defence would require US$1trn of investment between 2025 and 2027, even if substitute systems could be rushed into production.[93]

All this the US military does with expenditure equivalent to only 3.4% of annual GDP.[94] While the magnitude of its budget may not seem so, it is an extraordinarily cost-effective military. In *The Rise and Fall of the Great Powers* (1987), Paul Kennedy forecast the collapse of American power due to imperial overstretch.[95] And certainly the US chafes at the expansiveness of the international obligations it has undertaken. But that is a burden-sharing argument among allies, and a political question of national priorities, not a question of whether those obligations are financially unsustainable for the American economy to fund. The challenge of sustainability for the United States is not driven by international obligation or defence siphoning away resources needed for prosperity, as Kennedy projected, but rather domestic retirement and medical programmes (known in the US as 'entitlements' because their funding is automatic in the budgeting process) crowding out defence and other discretionary spending. Providing for the common defence, even the extended defence of the international order, is affordable for Americans.

V. Surveying the damage

These cultural, political, economic and military strengths propelled the US into becoming the hegemon of the international order in the twentieth century, and sustained it despite failures and mistakes of significant magnitude in both foreign and domestic policy. Whether in the current international environment the US can withstand the self-inflicted damage it is imposing is the question.

One of the most trenchant assessments of US power in the twenty-first century is by the journalist James Fallows, writing for *The Atlantic* in 2010. He ruminates on the fact that

> throughout the entirety of my conscious life, America has been on the brink of ruination, or so we have heard, from the launch of *Sputnik* through whatever is the latest indication of national falling apart or falling behind. Pick a year over the past half century, and I will supply an indicator of what at the time seemed a major turning point for the worse.[96]

Fallows uses Saclan Bercovitch's metaphor of the jeremiad (from Torah: Jeremiah prophesising doom because the Kingdom of Judah broke its covenant with God) as a way to highlight that the US is remarkably, uniquely good at identifying its failures and eventually becomes panic-stricken to correct them.[97] And it is certainly true that the US has overcome prior bouts of dysfunction and faltering prospects. So the question should perhaps be framed as why a society that has succeeded so well for so long should become unrecoverable now.

Several reasons suggest themselves: changes to the international order making repair of a beneficial system less likely; small decrements in powers destroying the network effects that make the US order 'sticky'; rabid partisanship and decreased accountability in federal governance making the US political system less responsive; and failure to fund the military power needed to sustain its obligations.

Assessments of the administration's first few months give a sense of the magnitude of the damage Trump's policies have produced. *The Economist* assesses that 'the story of [Trump's] first six months in office is how much his agenda has been consumed by his chaotic tariffs, a war on the civil service and attacks on the [Federal Reserve]'.[98] The newspaper elsewhere condemns the administration for 'junking universal principles for might-makes-right [which] repels friends without necessarily cowing foes', and notes that 'the more a country depends on America, the less dependable America is for it'.[99] Economist Adam Posen decries that 'Trump has switched the United States' role from global insurer to extractor of profit'.[100] Former CIA director William Burns describes the effect of Trump administration policies thus far as 'strategic self-immolation'.[101]

Michael Johnston, writing in *Foreign Affairs*, concludes that the Trump administration has

> embraced a style of governance in which power flows directly from a single leader, creating opportunities for personal deals to drive official decisions. [These dynamics threaten] free political and economic processes and can, eventually, become integral to the way the entire system functions – making it highly resistant to reform.[102]

Aggressive visa restrictions, deportations and arbitrary restrictions on federal funding have resulted in a 28% drop in arrivals of foreign college students since the start of the current administration.[103] Describing the 'new economic geography', Posen notes that

> Trump has threatened to block access to American markets on a broad scale; made the protections that come with military alliances explicitly dependent on the purchase of US weapons, energy, and industrial

products; required foreigners who want to operate businesses in the United States to make side payments to his personal priorities; and pressured Mexico, Vietnam, and other countries to drop Chinese industrial inputs or investment by Chinese companies. These acts are on a scale unprecedented in modern US governance.[104]

The only times the 'Economic Policy Uncertainty Index' for the US has topped 200 have been in Trump's first and second terms – and both times it crested at nearly 600 (the average hovers around 100).[105] This 'state capitalism with American characteristics' is spooking investors.[106] Benighted Federal Reserve Chair Jerome Powell announced that 'GDP growth has slowed notably in the first half of [2025], to a pace of 1.2%, roughly half the 2.5% pace in 2024'.[107] In December 2025, Powell acknowledged that goods inflation had increased as a result of tariffs.[108]

International reordering

Even if Fallows is correct about American regeneration, other countries – America's friends and America's enemies – need to leave it time to correct its mistakes, and there is no reason to believe that this time the US will be gifted sufficient time to do so. In fact, trends suggest quite the opposite.

China certainly seems to believe that the US is in terminal decline. While some committed Marxists have long argued to that effect, there are few enough committed Marxists in contemporary China. The argument really begins with the 2008 financial crisis and burgeons with 'domestic political dysfunction and the chaos of the Trump administration to the American military–political failures in Iraq and Afghanistan and the gross mishandling of the COVID-19 pandemic'.[109]

China's perception pairs with and perhaps motivates an increasingly aggressive Chinese foreign and defence policy.

China's defence spending increased at a rate of 10% per year between 2000 and 2016, and this rate has remained at 7% since then. It is tripling the size of its nuclear-weapons forces and acquiring weapons at rates of five to six times the US, and according to US Indo-Pacific Command commander Admiral Sam Paparo, Chinese air and maritime operations against Taiwan increased by 300% in 2024.[110] China's navy has 312 ships while the US navy has only 221, and China has 232 times – 232 *times!* – the shipbuilding capacity of the US.[111] Those trends portend ill both for deterring Chinese aggression and for winning a war of any significant duration.

Chinese Premier Xi Jinping has ordered the People's Liberation Army to be capable of recapturing Taiwan by 2027.[112] Chinese Communist Party (CCP) leaders' belief in the inevitability of US decline ought logically to cause China to spare itself the effort of fighting and instead bide its time and allow the US to corrode its own power; however, Xi could also judge the US to be sufficiently weak that China could succeed and move against US interests and allies in the region on a timeline that suits his domestic determinants. And seeing the way China has activated the antibodies against its own continued success with 'wolf-warrior' diplomacy, aggression against the Philippines, taking hostage Western businesspeople, stripping its own successful businesspeople of their companies, sealing an 'alliance without limits' with Russia as that country invaded Ukraine, and weaponising economic interdependence against virtually every country, China may have concerns about its own power trajectory that spur it towards more immediate action to restore the stature and territory it claims.

Chinese strategy appears focused on creating cleavages between the US and its regional partners in Asia. As Chinese military prowess threatens damage to the US homeland, the cost of the US extending deterrence rises substantially. It is unclear whether the Trump administration even believes in protecting Taiwan, since President Trump has said Taiwan needs to 'pay us for defense' if it expects US protection and claims US–China talks would be 'great for unification and peace' – the Defense Department's policy lead having testified that the prospect of China attacking Taiwan would not be an existential threat to the US, and the growing consensus among senior officials in both the Trump and former Biden administrations that Taiwan has become the provocateur in cross-strait relations.[113]

There is also urgency in Europe. One of the few fixed ideas Donald Trump seems to hold, and has held since the 1980s, is that America's allies are a drain on US power and resources – that they have taken and continue to take advantage of the US.[114] No amount of data or advocacy dents that belief. There appears to be little or no inter-agency process vetting policy proposals, as attested to by the cutting off again and then re-allowing again of sale of weapons to Ukraine in summer 2025. A Trump political appointee obtained Secretary of Defense Pete Hegseth's approval to stop provision of weapons on the grounds that those same weapons were necessary for US forces operating in the Pacific; the military's sound strategic advice that deterrence is indivisible and Ukraine's success important was ignored. Congressional and allied and public agitation began imposing a political price on the president, who disavowed any knowledge of the policy decision then began calling people outside his administration to test the political salience of his position and ultimately reversed course on the matter.[115] That is how the Trump administration functions and how it is likely to continue to function.

Russia's most recent invasion of Ukraine grinds into its fifth year with no evidence its million casualties have caused

Vladimir Putin to reduce the expansiveness of his war aims. Nor is there much evidence that President Trump is willing to put American power behind the defence of Ukraine's sovereignty over its internationally recognised territory, despite 'disappointment' with Putin and relenting on weapons provision to Ukraine, and the belief held by American allies in both Europe and Asia that preventing Russian success in Ukraine is important for deterring Chinese aggression against Taiwan.

All that is before the boorish behaviour towards allies as evidenced by the Oval Office meeting with Ukrainian President Volodymyr Zelenskyy and the resentments made clear in Vice President JD Vance's Munich Security Conference speech (both in February 2025), chats on the Signal messaging app among Trump cabinet officials, the outright threats to take territory by force from Denmark, Canada and Panama, and the sentiments expressed towards Europe in the US National Security Strategy of November 2025.[116] European leaders reliant on security guarantees are conceding linkage, accepting tariffs and other demoralising demands. The journalist Mark Sappenfield concludes, 'when relations with the US were at their worst, the EU's public statements were ones of confidence, even defiance. Now, there is a deflating sense that alliance with the US comes with humiliation.'[117]

En route to the NATO summit that had been ingeniously designed to minimise the risk of bad behaviour by President Trump – short duration; shiny object of a 5%-of-GDP defence-spending commitment; obsequiousness from the secretary general – he nevertheless called into question the bindingness of NATO's mutual-defence commitment, telling the press pool that it 'depends on your definition … There's numerous definitions of Article 5. You know that, right?'[118]

NATO leaders engineered a row-back at the summit's conclusion, with Trump publicly stating that his presence attested to US commitment to allied defence.[119] And he conceded that 'these people really love their countries … It's not a rip-off, and we're here to help them protect their country.'[120] But the sheer impetuousness with which President Trump and his administration approach solemn commitments on which allied security relies has for the first time in a generation inspired serious consideration of European defence absent the United States.[121]

Trump has also imposed a maelstrom of tariffs that, even if they do not collapse the global economy, have demonstrated stark evidence of American unreliability as an economic partner, even imposing tariffs on Canada and Mexico in violation of the United States–Mexico–Canada Agreement his administration concluded during his first term. US tariffs skyrocketed from an average of under 3% to over 9% and continue to climb.[122] As Canada's Prime Minister Mark Carney has said, 'the United States is beginning to monetize its hegemony'.[123]

The arrangement of the current international order with US power as its undergirding is what political scientists call 'sticky': existing patterns are resistant to change. What makes the American-led order sticky, as the great theorist of liberal order G. John Ikenberry robustly described, is that it became a 'Liberal Leviathan', built on a combination of commitment and restraint by the dominant power.[124] He theorises:

> Cooperative order is built around a basic bargain: the hegemonic state obtains commitments from secondary states to participate within the postwar order, and in return the hegemon places limits on the exercise of its power. The weaker states do not fear domination or abandonment – reducing the incentives to balance – and the leading state does not need to use its power assets to enforce order and compliance.[125]

Ikenberry demonstrates that 'it was the exercise of strategic restraint – made good by an open polity and binding institutions – more than the direct and instrumental exercise of hegemonic domination that ensured a cooperative and stable postwar order'.[126] That behaviour created a shared normative understanding, a common approach to problem-solving that allowed the American-led order to outlast the existence of the threat against which it had coalesced. It is that shared normative understanding that the US will comport itself with transparency and through consensual institutions that the Trump administration is rejecting.

The Economist describes Trump's strategy as 'capricious and confusing'.[127] To the extent there is a plumb line (doctrine is too generous a term) through Trump administration policy, it seems to envision a concert of great powers, where the strongest nations decide the fate of those less able to protect themselves. It is a nineteenth-century model of spheres of influence and mercantile trading, the international order so-called 'realists' have claimed was extant in every era.[128]

But the darkening mood especially among small and middle powers is the refutation of that school of international relations, because the countries that have enjoyed the experience of the American-led order feel its cooling temperature and fear the rupture of a storm. Those countries know other states would create or impose a different order. And it merits remembering, particularly for the US as it burns through international goodwill and undermines the international institutions it created, that the Athenians, who brazenly insisted that 'the strong do what they can and the weak suffer what they must', ultimately destroyed their sources of strength in the Peloponnesian wars.[129]

Much of Trump's policy appears to be so self-defeating as to constitute hegemonic suicide. The *Atlantic* sums up the approach as based on a belief that 'to remain superpowerful, the U.S. may need to temporarily stop superpowering'.[130] The lack of distinction between allies and adversaries is especially rattling those countries that contribute to upholding American power, and that are mainstays of international organisations. European Commission President Ursula von der Leyen, a former German defence minister, believes 'the West as we knew it no longer exists'.[131] *Die Zeit* newspaper describes Trump foreign policy in family-law terms as 'malicious abandonment'.[132]

Countries have begun to research how to secure their supply chains by skirting the US market because of tariffs, to establish trade in local currencies, and to join together in multilateral trading regimes that exclude the US. Trade is rising among all other countries, just not with the US.[133] It is of course true that Donald Trump did not begin the stagnation of global trade agreements (the failure of the Doha Round was evident by 2008, nine years before Trump took office), and politicians of both US political parties have been hostile to trade for several electoral cycles. But none have wielded tariff threats randomly and applied tariffs with the staggering severity – 500% in some cases – to which the Trump administration has subjected the global economic system. It portends the biggest jolt to the global trading system since the Smoot–Hawley Tariff Act of the 1930s.

Once American power ceases to be the reliable undergirding of the international order, countries will have to make other arrangements. To the extent there is strategic forethought in the Trump administration, it seems to be operating on the assumption that other countries have no alternative to conceding to US demands or making choices consistent with US interests and preferences.[134] This is, of course, untrue. Other states may not have better options, but they do have choices and may very well choose concessions to American adversaries out of the belief that the US either cannot be relied upon or is insufficiently different from or better than its adversaries.

The network effects of underwriting the international security and economic orders would seem insensitive to small defections such as lesser states opting out. But that turns out not to be true. Economic modelling can demonstrate that 'power does not grow in a straight line. It tends to shoot up as a hegemon's market share nears 100%.'[135] Defections from participation in the order will have outsized effects on Washington's ability to retain dominant international influence. And the United States is in no way prepared for an international order wherein it does not set the agenda, wherein other states decline to make its problems their problems and contribute to their solutions. The United States has seldom fought a war without other countries contributing on its side of the fight, yet that is the world the Trump administration is conjuring into existence.

Unfunny comedy

James Fallows had already in 2010 identified 'the American tragedy of the early 21st century: a vital and self-renewing culture that attracts the world's talent, and a governing system that increasingly looks like a joke'.[136] Congress has seized up through a combination of partisanship and performance art. As the post-Second World War American government expanded its remit in regulation and social-welfare programmes, legislation became more cumbersome (Trump's 'One Big Beautiful Bill', signed into law in summer 2025, was 1,116 pages long), and powers that had been exercised locally and often non-governmentally (like care for the poor) became federal responsibilities. Moreover, narrow electoral margins and increasingly gerrymandered political districts have made bipartisan legislating less frequent and incentivised parliamentary manoeuvrings that disrupted regular order and leeched authority from committees in both houses of Congress. The end of 'earmarks' that facilitated legislative compromises, ostensibly a win for transparency and reducing corruption, had the effect of further neutering the power of party leaders in Congress and thereby making it more difficult to pass legislation; as a result, the defence authorisation is the only piece of legislation guaranteed to pass, and even it has failed to pass on time in 11 of the last 13 years. Campaign-finance rulings by the courts coupled with partisan broadcasting have made every election campaign national in its fundraising and messaging – there is less local content even in local elections. Congress routinely spends money far in excess – trillions of dollars in excess – of that which it collects in tax receipts. All of this amounts to Congress being both less responsible and seen as less legitimate for solving the country's pressing political problems. The People's Republic of China is gaining traction internationally by cautioning against the chaotic inconsequentiality of American democracy.[137]

Despair over Congress is, of course, nothing new. Early twentieth-century newspaperman H.L. Mencken derided it as consisting of 'one-third, more or less, scoundrels; two-thirds, more or less, idiots; and three-thirds, more or less, poltroons' ('poltroon' being an archaic word for coward).[138] Mark Twain, who had worked as a Senate staffer, considered that 'there is no distinctly American criminal class except Congress'.[139] But Neil Postman's 1980s critique of American society 'amusing ourselves to death', turning politics into entertainment and thereby destroying accountability, 'narcotized by technological diversions', rings even truer in the age of TikTok, *The Apprentice* and other reality television.[140]

Since the foundation of the republic, Congress has done as much or as little as the American voters will let it get away with. It has shown itself capable of reform and moderation and possesses the tools to exert the powers enumerated for it in Article 1 of the Constitution. It is Congress failing to exercise its constitutional responsibility to negotiate broad-based consensus that has most destabilised the American political order in the Trump era. As Yuval Levin argues,

> Congress has to produce not only legislation but legitimacy. And although majority rule is essential to democratic legitimacy, majority power endangers minority rights and risks rendering the government unjust and therefore illegitimate. So legitimacy requires that majorities be broadened before they are empowered.[141]

That is manifestly not happening in the 119th (current) Congress, and any efforts at bipartisan problem-solving, as occurred in 2024 on border issues, get quashed by the Damoclean sword of Trump's threats to primary any Republican who votes for a bipartisan bill. Compounding the effects of a complacent Congress is a president who seems genuinely not to believe in the normative and even legal restraints that have governed the American presidency. Donald Trump is a twice-impeached convicted felon busily traducing the practices that have constrained the behaviour of his presidential predecessors, daring the courts to rebuke him, but attesting he would comply if they did.[142] That he was re-elected and continues to retain the support of 38% of the populace should not inspire confidence that the US political system will right itself.[143]

Killing the goose

The American economy has structural weaknesses and faces important challenges. The middle of the labour market has been hollowed out by automation.[144] Able-bodied men are opting out of work, and able-bodied women are increasingly following their lead.[145] Demographic decline is occurring in the United States as in most other advanced economies, just not as rapidly. And the national debt is a ticking time bomb of unfunded obligations of the money of succeeding generations. But the majority of dangers facing the American economy are self-inflicted and of recent vintage because they are the result of Trump administration policies.

As a topline figure, the combined effects of Trump's policies have caused the IMF to reduce its projections of US economic growth to just 2% for the coming year.[146] The Federal Reserve estimates only 1.2% growth, less than half its projection before Trump's election. Businesses are withdrawing their plans and projections because of the uncertainty Trump's policies are injecting into every sector.[147]

The randomness and severity of Trump's tariffs have dented the 'flight to safety' that US debt has historically enjoyed. The rate at which the US can attract investors for its deficit spending is getting steeper: Canada, China, France, Germany, Greece, Italy, Japan and South Korea now can issue bonds at lower interest rates than the US.[148] Trump's railing against Federal Reserve Chair Jerome Powell and threats to appoint a 'shadow chair' have called into question the continuing independence of the Federal Reserve.[149] J.P. Morgan's CEO Jamie Dimon has warned that

if we are not the pre-eminent military and the pre-eminent economy in 40 years, we will not be the reserve currency … People tell me we are enormously resilient. I agree with that. I think this time is different. This time we have to get our act together and do it very quickly.[150]

While the stock market remains complacent, signs are already beginning to accrue that trading partners and investors are rethinking reliance on and even exposure to the US economy.[151] Uncertainty associated with Trump administration policies coupled with attacks on the independence of the Federal Reserve, gargantuan deficit spending and erosion of the rule of law are all denting confidence in the US as a place to invest and do business. The dollar has fallen 10% since President Trump's inauguration.[152] Deutsche Bank cautions its clients that 'the safe haven properties of the dollar are being eroded … It is no longer hyperbole to say that the dollar's reserve status and broader dominant role is at least somewhat in question.'[153] The inverse relation between exchange rates and bond yields in the US has begun mirroring the pattern of developing economies; the dollar weakening with stock volatility suggests that dollar dominance, in the view of *The Economist*, is 'bruised – but the damage is not worsening'.[154] Yet.

Adam Tooze identifies the 'dollar trap', which is that since 2008, 'the network of Advanced Economy non-bank financial institutions centered above all around the US Treasury market has new dynamics and new risks'. Financial transfers are circumventing banks and running through international portfolio investors utilising bond markets. That is, even as the US economy grows riskier, other advanced economies are growing more reliant on the dollar due to the choices of private lenders – they now account for more than half of all foreign holdings of treasuries.[155] Privatised dollar holdings do not have the political and security relationships that inhibit a run by states, and are therefore more easily spooked into selling quickly, requiring central-bank interventions. To quote the BIS, 'financial instability could originate or be amplified by liquidity stresses'.[156] The US system is therefore more brittle than others, more subject to bursting bubbles and financial crashes.

China is attempting to put its economy out of reach of US policies, crafting trade relationships in yuan with Brazil, Russia, South Korea and petrostates of the Gulf. The government of China is also loaning yuan to central banks in Argentina and Pakistan, supplanting the US role as lender of last resort.[157] Potential alternatives to dollar clearing are proliferating: China created a Cross-Border Interbank Payment System to process payments in yuan, and after Russia was excluded from the SWIFT payments system, it developed an alternative – the System for Transfer of Financial Messages – with the added advantage of providing secrecy for clients (something SWIFT does not do).[158]

Not only are adversaries moving to shield themselves from the reach of the US, but allies are as well:

> It is a split screen that is becoming typical. On one side, the United States sows uncertainty as it blows up weeks of painstaking negotiations and escalates tariff threats. On the other, the 27-nation European Union and other American trading partners are forging closer ties, laying the groundwork for a global trading system that revolves less and less around an increasingly fickle United States.[159]

Both the United Kingdom and Canada have pulled into closer alignment with the EU.[160] Japan and South Korea, two treaty allies of the United States whose sovereignty and security rely on American military power, are mooting a trilateral trade agreement with China, a state that poses direct threats to them both.[161] As Nicholas Grossman has argued, 'the impact of Trump's hostility to the world isn't deglobalization; it's de-Americanization'.[162] And while the Trump administration chooses not to connect issues, others will. As Andreas Bauer has said, 'the negative is that the long-term trust in the US is extremely undermined ... The coming generation of EU leaders will remember these situations.'[163]

Nor, for all its fizziness and dynamism, is the continued primacy of the US technology sector a sure thing. Trump administration attacks on universities, draconian cuts to scientific grants, and the surveillance and harassment of foreigners risks destroying the scientific empire as even three-quarters of *American* scientists consider leaving the United States.[164]

At present, the US continues to dominate frontier technologies, but Trump administration policies that scare away foreign talent and challenge research funding threaten this.[165] By contrast, China's long-term research investment could allow it to pull ahead in crucial technologies such as AI and bioprinting.[166]

In absolute terms, the US could face a 'second China shock', whereby China surpasses the US intellectual and innovation ecosystem.[167] Kyle Chan argues that

> the battle for A.I. supremacy will be fought not between the United States and China but between high-tech Chinese cities like Shenzhen and Hangzhou. Chinese factories around the world will reconfigure supply chains with China at the centre, as the world's pre-eminent technological and economic superpower.[168]

The avarice of US companies could also spell doom for US economic primacy as 'the traditional platform economy is being reshaped as commercial platforms and government institutions merge into a monstrous hybrid of business monopoly and state authority'.[169] That is, leaders of technology innovations that come to have network effects are pairing with government in the Trump era for subsidies and market protections that allow domestic-market dominance but are likely to result in inferior technologies and products over time as they are shielded from competition. This dynamic would replicate the disadvantages of Chinese state-owned or -controlled businesses, but with the American twist of worsening products and customer service.

Sleight of the mailed fist

The Trump administration is attempting to lay claim to president Ronald Reagan's mantra of 'peace through strength'.[170] It trumpets the president's assertiveness in attacking Iran's uranium-enrichment programme and Ansarullah (Houthi) forces in the Red Sea; the passage of a trillion-dollar defence budget; regaining control of the Panama Canal; 'ensuring career diplomats reflect the foreign policy of the United States at all times';[171] and building a 'golden dome' of missile defences over the United States. Yet many of these claims are obviously inflated or entail unacknowledged fragilities. Just to take two:

- The trillion-dollar defence budget relies on a one-time congressionally added US$150bn increase. The president's budget actually represents a US$31.5bn cut from the final Biden administration budget.[172] Brinkmanship by the Office of Management and Budget to break the parity between defence and non-defence spending is destroying bipartisan support for defence, making continuing resolutions or utilisation of reconciliation legislation more likely than the regular order of congressional oversight and on-time budget passage.
- The golden-dome missile defence is directed to be initially deployed within the three remaining years of Trump's term in office.[173] That will necessitate pulling

back into the US all its air-defence systems currently deployed in allied countries, and stationing close to US shores all sea-based *Aegis* defensive systems. In order to marginally improve protections for US territory that will still be insufficient to prevent its principal adversaries from successfully striking it, the US will need to denude front-line allies of defences that are deterring attacks on them.

America's closest friends and allies have avoided overt ructions with the US over trade and other issues because of their reliance on the US for security. But the damage of disrespect is accruing, as reflected in this comment from Danish politician Claus Hjort Frederiksen:

> For me – a person who has been trusting the US all these years since then – it's very hard to experience that it doesn't mean anything anymore that we had fought alongside the US in Afghanistan, in Iraq and many other places, that suddenly we are nothing.[174]

A 2025 survey showed that 51% of EU citizens now actually consider President Trump 'an enemy of Europe', and the sentiment is strongest in the countries that have historically had the highest regard for the US.[175] The next time the US goes to war, it may be forced to fight without allied soldiers alongside it.

The American military cannot remain a global power projector without assistance from friendly states. Sending US forces around the world requires overflight rights, transit through the Panama and Suez canals, agreements on port usage in foreign countries, existence of and access to US bases in foreign countries, and drawing rights on fuel and even ammunition from other countries. Intelligence-sharing by allied governments is essential in informing US military operations. All of these advantages are routine practices now, but all depend on governments' willingness to allow the US to operate in and above their territory, and cooperation from their military and intelligence personnel. And in free societies – the countries that are America's closest friends and on whose cooperation its military prowess most depends – that requires public support of the kind the Trump administration is energetically destroying.

As I wrote in *Foreign Affairs* in July 2025, the Trump administration

> takes for granted all the benefits that a cooperative approach has yielded, and cannot envision a future in which other countries opt out of the existing U.S.-led international order or construct a new one that would be antagonistic to American interests. Yet those are precisely the outcomes the Trump administration is hastening.[176]

Not only might allies not answer the US call to participate in wars it fights, but they are also moving to coordinate their own defences by excluding it. German Chancellor Friedrich Merz has said 'my absolute priority will be to strengthen Europe as quickly as possible so that, step by step, we can really achieve independence from the United States'.[177]

Trump's calling into question NATO's Article 5 mutual-defence pledge led the UK and France to commit in the July 2025 Northwood Declaration to coordinate their nuclear planning and extend the perimeter of their nuclear considerations to security in all of Europe.[178] France refuses to coordinate nuclear policy within NATO but sees the need to extend nuclear deterrence for Europe because other European states can no longer rely upon the US guarantee.

The US stepped back from convening the Ukraine Defence Contact Group of 51 defence ministers meeting monthly to coordinate and provide assistance to Ukraine, and shut off weapons deliveries and intelligence feeds, leading customers of US defence companies to conclude they needed both alternate suppliers and rapid development of indigenous defence-industrial capacity.[179] The EU's Readiness 2030 plan would create a US$164bn fund for purchases of weapons produced in European states, with particular emphasis on air- and missile-defence systems, artillery, ammunition, drones, equipment for use in cyber and electronic warfare, and 'strategic enablers' like air-to-air refuelling – all things the US has previously provided to NATO's common defence.

Inter-operability is a major advantage in coalition warfare, and reliance on US practices and equipment has provided the basis for inter-operability not just among NATO forces but also of US military coalitions everywhere in the world. The divergence of European militaries from NATO standardisation agreements will diminish the fighting effectiveness of US-led coalitions. Additionally, as sales of European – to include Ukrainian – equipment increasingly compete with US arms sales, standards for equipment may develop for countries beyond Europe, and the US may not be able to synchronise its own equipment with these standards, further reducing inter-operability.

Trump's policies are also harming the culture of the American military and its positive relationship with the broader American public. Castigating 'the generals', pardoning soldiers convicted by courts martial even of war crimes, appointing to senior civilian positions in the Pentagon people drummed out of military service for insubordination (or worse), holding political rallies on military bases and calling on troops to boo rival politicians, dismissing competent commanders, and sending troops to participate in domestic policing and immigrant detentions and deportations, all attack the non-political nature and institutional values of the American military in ways that are likely to squander enormous amounts of talent, harm recruitment and retention, and create friction within the military itself.[180]

Reverse polarisation

In 2010, James Fallows argued that

> the simplest measure of whether a culture is dominant is whether outsiders want to be part of it … The American advantage here is broad and atmospheric, but it also depends on two specific policies that, in my view, are the absolute pillars of American strength: continued openness to immigration, and a continued concentration of universities that people around the world want to attend.[181]

Both of these are specific priority targets of Trump administration policies. Rates of immigration and college applications from foreign students are declining significantly, depriving the US of those talented individuals so important to the dynamism not just of its economy, but of its society.

Figures on foreign attitudes and tourism are likely leading indicators of the effect of Trump's policies. Just four months into President Trump's second term, international support for the US had dramatically dipped: according to the 2025 Democracy Perception Index, the majority of the world now views the US negatively, marking a significant decline in popularity since 2024. The US is less well thought of than China in most countries worldwide (including nearly every country in the Western Hemisphere), and President Trump (at 27% positive and 58% negative perception) is less well thought of than Xi Jinping (32% positive and 31% negative).[182]

The capriciousness and danger of immigration enforcement by the Trump administration have caused tourism to plummet.[183] The US Travel Association estimates that the US will lose US$21bn in travel-related revenue in 2025 if current trends continue, citing issues such as excessive visa wait times.[184] According to Arun Ryan of Oxford Economics, 'Trump administration "posturing and policy" tied to issues like border security and tariffs on long-standing trade partners have created "sentiment-headwinds" among would-be travelers … Perceptions of the US matter'.[185]

Many have raised serious concerns that long-standing US norms against self-enrichment are at risk of erosion. Extensive reporting alleges that the Trump presidency has appeared at times to blur the boundary between public authority and the private financial interests of the president and his family. Many commentators see the scale of these possible conflicts of interest as unmatched in recent US politics.[186]

The most incisive assessment of the damage being done to American power was delivered posthumously by the originator of the idea of 'soft power' (the magnetic attraction of culture) Joseph S. Nye, Jr., along with Robert Keohane:

> Wise American policy would maintain, rather than disrupt, patterns of interdependence that strengthen American power, both the hard power derived from trade relationships and the soft power of attraction. The continuation of Trump's current foreign policy would weaken the United States and accelerate the erosion of the international order that since World War II has served so many countries well – most of all, the United States. … Trump's measures are misplaced, since they

attack those forms of globalization that are largely good for the United States and the world while failing to counter those that are bad. On balance, globalization has enhanced American power, and Trump's assault on it only enfeebles the United States.[187]

All this makes it difficult to refute Soviet émigré and American writer Gary Shteyngart when he concludes that 'I was born to one dying superpower and am now living in another'.[188]

VI. Denouement?

The history of great powers is that they tend eventually to decline and fall, although across varying time spans and sometimes due more to external shock than to internal errors. But probably no dominant power in history has done so much damage to the sources of its own power in such a short time as has the United States in its recent era.

Of the great empires, Rome took a century to fall (and centuries more if you count the endurance of the eastern, or Byzantine, extension).[189] The Mexica terrorised tributary tribes across Mesoamerica for 190 years before Hernán Cortés's horses, steel and alliance-building quickly precipitated the surrender of their dominance – but their collapse was largely forced on them by superior technologies rather than their own choices.[190] China's Ming dynasty succumbed to a combination of military and peasant mutinies in about 15 years, with remnants clinging on to power for about another 20 years.[191] The Inca of South America held out against Portuguese pressure for 40 years. Britain contracted from being 'an empire on which the sun never set' to being just the United Kingdom by shedding its colonies and hegemony across 80 years.[192] The Ottoman Empire endured upheaval across decades before collapsing in the aftermath of the First World War.[193]

Comparisons to the decline of relative US power may depend on when you 'start the clock'. If the 2001 American response to al-Qaeda's attacks and the subsequent catastrophic choices on invading Iraq in 2003 are the starting point, then we are now a quarter of a century into this process. Both Athens and Sparta destroyed their sources of power contending against each other across the 27 years of the Peloponnesian War. Sweden's eighteenth-century dominance of northern Europe collapsed with its loss to Russia across the 21 years of the Great Northern War. This kind of time frame would also include twentieth-century Imperial Japan, which invaded Manchuria in 1931 and was forced into unconditional surrender to American forces with the atomic-bomb attacks on Hiroshima and Nagasaki in 1945.

Collapse can occur even more rapidly. If President Trump's first term in office were the starting point, the destruction of American power would extend across the past nine years, putting some historical empires into the mix.[194] The Comanche, who controlled more territory than the United States until 1873, were driven onto reservations within four years.[195] Nazi Germany's Third Reich commenced in 1933 and ended with the Soviet Union and the United States meeting at the Elbe River in 1945.

Even if the stopwatch begins only with the second Trump term in 2025, there are other examples of even more rapid destruction. Alexander the Great's Macedonian-ruled empire, which extended all the way to India, was divided up by his successors immediately after his death in 323 BCE. The Mayan civilization disappeared fast in the ninth century for reasons and by means still inexplicable.[196] In perhaps the most alarming comparison, the Soviet Union's ignominious end could be clocked from the coup attempt against Mikhail Gorbachev in

August 1991 to dissolution by December the same year.[197] Still, the USSR had been in dire financial straits for some years due to a shift in the global economic environment: the price of oil, on which it depended, had shrunk in the 1980s.

What is extraordinary about the contemporary American example, however, is how conducive were the international and domestic circumstances for US power to continue to dominate its historical moment. Nor was the destruction externally determined by losing a war, the death of a leader, or some technological advancement leaving it incapable of succeeding. In July 2025, the historian Margaret MacMillan argued that

> the striking lack of historical precedents for [the Trump administration's] behaviour does not suggest a clever Machiavellian policy to enhance American power; rather, it shows a United States acting against its own interests in bewildering fashion, undermining one of the key sources of that power.[198]

The Trump administration's choices are the motive force behind the rapid contraction of American power: we are doing it to ourselves. Just as Abraham Lincoln prophesised in 1838, 'if destruction be our lot, we must ourselves be its author and finisher. As a nation of freemen, we must live through all time, or die by suicide.'[199]

So collapse of American power due to its electoral choices and the inability or unwillingness of its distributed power structures to restrain President Trump and his policies is the way to bet your money. At present, it feels like this time may be different: that hubris will overcome the jeremiad tendency of previous American renewals and that too many Americans will not notice the power collapse around them until it is too late. This collapse could well be signalled or catalysed by a crisis in the international economic structure and/or a major war.

But it is important to acknowledge that there may be other, less likely pathways, including continued American resilience and renewal, and perhaps even a relative strengthening of the US within the international order (or more likely international disorder).

The political scientist Michael Beckley argues that 'American dysfunction has had remarkably little effect on American power, which remains resilient and, in some respects, has even grown'. Beckley is right to identify this as

> the paradox of American power: the United States is a divided country, perpetually perceived as in decline, yet it consistently remains the wealthiest and most powerful state in the world – leaving competitors behind. How can such dominance emerge from disorder? The answer is that the United States' main assets – its vast land, dynamic demographics, and decentralized political institutions – also create severe liabilities.[200]

One does not have to accept Beckley's conclusion elsewhere that the US will become a 'rogue superpower' to acknowledge that what has made the US dynamic and successful may keep it so, even with the chaos premium Trump administration policies are forcing the US and other states to pay.[201] The wellsprings of American power are strong. Moreover, dominance is a relative index, not an absolute one. The US can perhaps make choices that impoverish itself relative to its prior trajectory of prosperity and leave it less secure than previously without vanquishing its dominant role in the international order. For not only is America strong, despite many recent self-inflicted liabilities, but many of its rivals have serious weaknesses of their own.

For American dominance to come to an end, either an unlikely generalised international chaos would need to ensue or other contenders would need to emerge as rule-givers and enforcers in the international order. China is the obvious replacement, given the size of its economy and its clear ambition to change the existing rules. But although the potential for Chinese technological leadership remains, it is also possible that the wave of Chinese power may already have crested.[202] The CCP is banking on technology innovation and exports to power its success, and while so far it has done remarkably well, it has also now activated antibodies in the form of tech restrictions from other advanced economies. Its model of property-sector and infrastructure investment has reached its limit, now producing less return on investment, creating real fragility for the economy and portending structural slowdown. Consumer and investor confidence have been battered, especially by the CCP's draconian and disastrous COVID policy, and do not appear to be recovering.[203] Government goals for economic growth are increasingly fantastical; in reality, after accounting for official dissimulation, Chinese growth rates are perhaps little more than US ones.[204] Yanzhong Huang calculates that 'the GDP gap between United States and China widened significantly from $5 trillion in 2021 to nearly $10 trillion by 2023'.[205] Even some prominent Chinese commentators consider it wishful thinking that China could replace the US.[206]

Nor, for all its belligerence towards Taiwan and the Philippines, support for Russia's war effort in Ukraine and establishment of a military base in Djibouti, does China appear willing to undertake security obligations in the way or to anywhere near the degree that has extended American power throughout the international order.[207] China's foreign minister may have admitted that China cannot accept Russia's losing in Ukraine because that would allow the US to concentrate its attention on Asia.[208] But despite that and the so-called Sino-Russian 'alliance without limits' and significant indirect economic and technological contributions to Russia's war effort, China has been very cautious about overtly assisting Russia's war in Ukraine and has declined to recognise Russian territorial claims there.[209]

Russians may aspire to be part of a troika of great powers, and Donald Trump's flattery of them encourages the fiction and assists their aggression, but Russia has nowhere near the political, economic or technological power to qualify as a superpower. The Russian economy appears near to exhausting the growth that policy latitude and oil exports allowed.[210] For all of Russia's rhetoric about being at war with NATO and the West, it has barely broken even a smaller and largely Soviet-designed military in Ukraine; it could in no way succeed in fighting the Polish, Finnish or French armed forces, much less the US or the collective NATO alliance. In summer 2025, the US Army's senior officer in Europe publicly reminded Russia of the power differential, assessing that NATO forces could seize Russian Kaliningrad 'in a timeframe that is unheard of'.[211] Nor, for all the developing world's aggravation at Western double standards of caring desperately about Ukraine but not about wars affecting them, are states enthusiastic about legitimating Russia's violations of Ukrainian sovereignty. The likelihood is vanishingly small that Russia can even recover the economic and political stature it had before invading Ukraine. It is more likely to become a snarlingly unsuccessful declining power than a driving force internationally. Of course, Russia could be included in the great-power club by Sino-American fiat, despite not objectively meriting inclusion.

A great-power condominium is also unlikely, despite President Trump's evident attraction to authoritarian leaders and flirtation with grand bargains that would betray American allies. Tempted as he might be, Trump was played by China in his first term (during which China promised but failed to purchase US products in agreed quantities), and is already being caterwauled by critics in the US for his 'TACO' (Trump Always Chickens Out) approach to imposing any costs on China (or Russia, for that matter).[212] Domestic backlash over mooted peace deals with Russia over the objections of Ukraine reveals the limits of an authoritarian order in which the US participates.[213] Even if Trump could garner the domestic backing for averting American eyes from the clashing values between democratic and authoritarian governments, the US and Chinese economies are in such direct competition on their leading edges it is likely to prevent a political covenant over the heads and objections of America's allies and security partners.

If not a singular hegemon or great-power condominium, an alternative international order could conceivably – although improbably – emerge through cooperation by the middle and small powers whose interests align: Australia, Canada, the EU, Japan, Mexico, Singapore, South Korea and the UK.[214] Together, their economic power surpasses that of the US, and they have leading regional roles that could reinforce each other. Their combined military strength could not overpower the US, but it would be a significant deterrent to US aggression. Although responses to arbitrary tariff actions by the US suggest the leading middle powers are hesitant to openly break with or provoke the US, there have already been some efforts to coordinate responses, and to threaten to establish an international order without the US at its core. The EU completed trade negotiations with Mercosur, and is considering arrangements with Canada and the 12 countries – including both the United States' immediate neighbours – in the Comprehensive and Progressive Agreement for Trans-Pacific Trade Partnership (CPTPP). Japan and South Korea, two countries deeply reliant on US security guarantees, are even considering moving beyond friendly countries to China in order to lock in greater trade reliability than the US is now providing.[215]

Creating a common front would dramatically increase the costs to the US of its erratic and unilateral policies. Such a grouping could conceivably utilise international organisations to hem in US power. But there is little evidence that the middle powers could surmount the difficulties of creating a common approach, and to the extent that they have already cooperated, it has been to placate the US rather than confront it. The countries of the ideational West have a long way to go before they become a bulwark against American power; and if, as constitutionally required, Donald Trump's term in office concludes in January 2029, many if not most are likely to play for time rather than undertake the extraordinary exertions necessary to cauterise their security and economies from American power.

The US is the country best insulated against international upheaval, having won the geopolitical lottery of abundant resources, an enormous internal market, Canada and Mexico as benign neighbours, and fewer reasons than most previous empires to venture beyond its own borders. Being largely its own market also suggests it could bring down the international order without bringing immediate calamity to itself – although financing its deficit spending opens a major vulnerability to autarchic functioning of its economy.

American risk tolerance makes the country uniquely resilient in times of upheaval. As James Fallows concludes, 'what is obvious from outside the country is how exceptional it is in its powers of renewal: America is always in decline, and is always about to bounce back'.[216] So the cultural tolerance for risk may make the US better able to withstand and adapt to a time of economic and technological change. This would not serve as vindication of the policies of the Trump administration, but rather their refutation:

the elements that have made America exceptional would once again have allowed it to thrive where others may have perished.

There is a more positive possible variant of this outcome, in which the US political system (and American international dominance) does not just 'muddle through' but eventually enjoys a period of renewal. Herman Wouk in *The Caine Mutiny* describes the US Navy in terms that have often been applied to the American system of government: 'a master plan designed by geniuses for execution by idiots'.[217] The founders were fearful of just about every malaise that could befall the nascent republic, and built into the structures of governance just about every conceivable protection. And while they fretted that the republic could not withstand failure of civic virtue, ambitious scoundrels were not unknown even in their time: Aaron Burr plotted nearly successfully during the founding generation to sever the bonds of the nascent republic's political union. Burr was assisted by General James Wilkinson, the senior officer in the army, who was a Spanish agent for the entirety of his 12 years in command.[218] President Thomas Jefferson's prosecution of Burr for treason was derailed by an even stronger political adversary, the chief justice of the US Supreme Court, John Marshall, establishing the tightly constrained American definition of treason. Ambition counteracting ambition, just as James Madison envisioned.

In this optimistic pathway, the pendulum swings back: violation of domestic political norms eventually produces a backlash; after the midterm elections of 2026, the policies of the Trump administration are checked and scrutinised more effectively thanks to opposition control of Congress and a more assertive judicial branch; the various institutions and groupings within civil society prove more successful in their own efforts to combat illiberal trends; President Trump leaves office peacefully in 2029 and his successor pledges not only to restore the previous norms of political behaviour but perhaps even to restrict the power of the presidency. At the time of writing in 2025, however, this Madisonian outcome appears grimly unlikely; the result of the 2026 midterm elections will give a strong indication as to its redemptive plausibility.

There is an even less likely possibility to which some remain attracted. In this scenario, Trump administration policies strengthen the United States by scraping the barnacles off the American ship of state. The argument goes that shedding obligations to states that free-ride off American power; refusing to continue funding international organisations that undercut American policies; frightening allies into more equitable burden-sharing; stripping the American military of ancillary duties and social policies that distract from fighting and winning the nation's wars; simplifying and thereby deconflicting the political objectives military force is expected to achieve; using military force to prevent emergent threats without being pulled into state-building; resuscitating domestic manufacturing; shielding American businesses from predatory state-financed foreign competition; brushing back courts that issue nationwide injunctions on matters better fought out in political channels; rolling back administrative regulation; securing the border and putting immigration on more politically acceptable footing; intimidating Congress and the courts from constraining executive power – could all result in a stronger United States.[219]

In such a configuration, if it came to pass, the US could prove stampedingly successful. Nor do President Trump's policies need to be purposeful to that end, or cease to work against each other (as tariffs and the strength of the dollar do), to propel the US to continued international dominance. Polities and economies are open, complex systems with numerous variables that re-weight and interact in ways that produce evolutionary outcomes. The things Trump has got destructively wrong could yet result in beneficial outcomes as people and markets figure out how to take advantage of new developments.

This would produce a different kind of order from the post-war liberal international order, but it could be less chaotic than disorder and likely still preferable to the wholly illiberal order on offer from the posited Sino-Russo-North Korean-Iranian order. And that 'axis of authoritarians' is not proving particularly solid, given how little assistance the other states provided to Iran as Israel collapsed the strategic depth Tehran had purchased by fomenting Hamas, Hizbullah and the Houthis, and put the survival of Iran's nuclear programme and even its leadership at risk.

Internationally, the US benefits from two exorbitant privileges in addition to dollar centrality: the adroitness of its allies, and the paucity of good alternatives. As demonstrated by former Japanese prime minister Abe Shinzo's masterful management of President Trump in his first term, the 2025 NATO summit avoiding Trump repudiating mutual defence or withdrawing US troops from Europe, and the EU's July 2025 sleight-of-hand trade agreement (promising future benefits unlikely to be delivered), American allies are beginning to make shrewd calculations about how much American nonsense to put up with in order to retain their security and prosperity in an American-dominated order, at least for a transition period while they strengthen their defences. The NATO allies are especially adept at buying time by smoothing over contradictory impulses: for example, the 1967 Harmel Report embraced the 'dual-track' policy of deterrence and detente, papering over France's withdrawal from the integrated military command; the 1979 'double-track' decision stipulated the deployment of intermediate-range nuclear weapons while negotiating their elimination; and this most recent elegant sleight of hand agreed to more than double defence spending by 2035 (when actually only 3.5% will go towards military improvements). That tolerance and skilful navigation is premised on an assumption that detrimental US policies and irascible US leaders can be both transitory and subject to influence. Short of full-on collapse of the US political system into authoritarianism, those assumptions by Western countries are likely to hold and sufficiently blur the disagreements to once again muddle through unpropitious circumstances imposed by the US.

Nor is China, the only real contender for creating an alternative order, so far excelling at capitalising on US mistakes. The Belt and Road Initiative (BRI), which looked so ruthlessly strategic when China was advancing loans the Bretton Woods institutions and Western governments would not, has now positioned China as the world's largest creditor, and for loans unlikely to ever be repaid: in 2022, 60% of China's BRI loans were to countries with payment in arrears, in default, engaged in restructuring programmes or at war.[220] It turns out the assessments by traditional lenders were correct, and China is shackled to infrastructure that failed to shift global trade patterns. The Chinese government will also not risk convertibility of its currency, a necessity to supplant the dollar as the international order's major currency, or provide the forward-looking guidance that allows businesses time to position themselves. Economist Martin Wolf concludes that 'the difficulty is that, however unsatisfactory the hegemon might be, the alternatives look worse'.[221]

All that said, the 'Trump resetting American power' argument fails to acknowledge the enormous costs such an approach entails. Ignoring (or, worse yet, continuing to encourage) aggression will tempt revanchist states, requiring more military effort by the US. Collapsing the international order will throw sand in the gears not just of other countries' economies, but of the US economy as well; at the same time it will dramatically increase the difficulty and cost of advancing American interests. If the dollar ceases to be a reliable repository of value, the US will not be able to finance domestic deficit spending. If allies cease to be enamoured with American power, the US will have to operate without their assistance, politically and militarily. If American immigration policies become so restrictive and deportations so repugnant, talent will no longer irrigate American businesses and universities, drying up both its scientific and cultural products. Once destroyed, the trust that underlies the post-1945 American order will take decades to reconstitute.

The Trump administration has ushered in a time of testing the risk tolerance of American culture, the ingenuity and strength of the American political system, the dynamic economy it engenders, and the international order it crafted after the Second World War. The Trump phenomenon is a maelstrom intended to rip the US free from obligations the country voluntarily agreed to be constrained by. Whether the American order can withstand the entropic forces Trump and his supporters relish unleashing is as yet unclear, but even if it proves able to do so, the reputational and economic costs Trump's policies are already imposing are incredibly damaging. Whether other countries will tolerate these forces or move to constrain them has begun to be tested. That Trump's policies will of necessity reduce the wellsprings of American power is virtually certain. No matter how much battering those wellsprings are being subjected to, they have heretofore proven remarkably resilient. That, of course, does not mean they will prove adequate to surmount the reckless determination of the Trump administration to reconfigure both the US domestic political space and the international order from which the US has drawn so much benefit.

If the wellsprings of American exceptionalism should falter, the choices Americans have made will prove of historic consequence. They may even end up paired by historians with the collapse of the Soviet Union in pace and significance of self-destruction.

NOTES

1   Others have considered similar ideas such as 'superpower suicide'; for example, see Rebecca Lissner and Mira Rapp-Hooper, 'Trump Is Forcing the World Into a New Era of Disorder', *New York Times*, 22 October 2025, https://www.nytimes.com/2025/10/22/opinion/trump-xi-summit-world-economy.html.

2   Jonathan Wilson, 'The History of Sport, Nazi Football, and World Cups', The Rest Is History podcast, 20 August 2025, at 10:06 in the podcast.

3   Donald E. Pease, 'American Exceptionalism', Oxford Bibliographies, 27 June 2018, https://www.oxfordbibliographies.com/display/document/obo-9780199827251/obo-9780199827251-0176.xml.

4   'John Winthrop's "City Upon a Hill," 1630', text of a sermon at Gilder-Lehrman Institute of American History, 2013, https://www.gilderlehrman.org/sites/default/files/inline-pdfs/Winthrop%27s%20City%20upon%20a%20Hill.pdf.

5   'Remarks from Colin Powell, U.S. Secretary of State', World Economic Forum, 26 January 2003, https://web.archive.org/web/20050223091222/http://www.weforum.org/site/homepublic.nsf/Content/Remarks+from+Colin+Powell,+US+Secretary+of+State.

6   Barack Obama, quoted in Michael Barone, 'How Has American Exceptionalism Fared Under Obama?', *National Review*, 15 January 2016, https://www.nationalreview.com/2016/01/american-exceptionalism-under-obama/.

7   John McCain, quoted in Aaron Korewa, 'Remembering Senator John McCain's Message in Munich', McCain Institute, 10 February 2020, https://www.mccaininstitute.org/resources/blog/remembering-senator-john-mccains-message-in-munich/.

8   Geir Lundestad, 'Empire by Invitation? The United States and Western Europe, 1945–1952', *Journal of Peace Research*, vol. 23, no. 3, September 1986, p. 263.

9   Walt Whitman, *Song of Myself, 52*, poets.org, https://poets.org/poem/song-myself-52. The poem is in the public domain.

10 This view was famously articulated by president Bill Clinton in his 1993

inaugural address, but had been expressed by several earlier American leaders, including presidents Dwight D. Eisenhower and Abraham Lincoln.

11 United States Census Bureau, 'New Vintage 2021 Population Estimates Available for the Nation, States and Puerto Rico', 21 December 2021, https://www.census.gov/newsroom/press-releases/2021/2021-population-estimates.html; and Mary van Beusekom, 'Survey Reveals Growing American Distrust in Vaccines for COVID, Other Infectious Diseases', University of Minnesota Center for Infectious Disease Research and Policy, 29 August 2024, https://www.cidrap.umn.edu/covid-19/survey-reveals-growing-american-distrust-vaccines-covid-other-infectious-diseases. The three US-produced vaccines were those made by Moderna, Novavax and Pfizer; the latter used mRNA technology developed by BioNTech, a German firm (itself founded by scientists of Turkish origin).

12 Peter Drucker, quoted in 'Culture Eats Strategy for Breakfast', Daily Agile, https://dailyagile.com/culture-eats-strategy-for-breakfast/.

13 Frederick Jackson Turner, 'The Significance of the Frontier in American History', *Proceedings of the State Historical Society of Wisconsin*, 14 December 1893.

14 David M. Kennedy, preface to Gordon Wood, *Empire of Liberty: A History of the Early Republic, 1789–1815* (Oxford: Oxford University Press, 2009), p. 8 (ebook).

15 Bertha Ann Reuter, *Anglo-American Relations During the Spanish–American War* (New York: Macmillan, 1924), p. 2.

16 Even many members of the 574 Native American tribes do not live in the territory of their ancestors, forced by other Native tribes or the federal government, or lured by better circumstances, to move to other locations.

17 Research by George Borjas for the National Bureau of Economic Research demonstrates that 'about half of the economic status of one immigrant generation persists into the next, a relationship that has remained stable over the past several decades'. See George J. Borjas, 'Making It in America: Social Mobility in the Immigrant Population', National Bureau of Economic Research, Working Paper 12088, March 2006, http://www.nber.org/papers/w12088.pdf.

18 'Los Angeles Unified School District by the Numbers', Los Angeles Almanac, https://www.laalmanac.com/education/ed721.php.

19 Wood, *Empire of Liberty*, p. 15.

20 Thomas Jefferson, 'Extract from Thomas Jefferson to Lafayette', 26 December 1820, Jefferson Quotes and Family Letters, Thomas Jefferson Foundation, https://tjrs.monticello.org/letter/386.

21 Dennis C. Rasmussen, *Fears of a Setting Sun: The Disillusionment of America's Founders* (Princeton, NJ: Princeton University Press, 2021), p. 2.

22 'The Federalist No. 1', Founders Online, US National Archives and Records Administration, 27 October 1787, https://founders.archives.gov/documents/Hamilton/01-04-02-0152.

23 Kori Schake, *Safe Passage: The Transition from British to American Hegemony* (Cambridge, MA: Harvard University Press, 2016), pp. 135–6.

24 Wood, *Empire of Liberty*, p. 254.

25 Matthew Arnold, *Discourses in America*, Project Gutenberg, p. 66, https://www.gutenberg.org/ebooks/44919.

26 Turner, 'The Significance of the Frontier in American History'.

27 John Gramlich, 'What the Data Says About Gun Deaths in the U.S.', Pew Research Center, 5 March 2025, https://www.pewresearch.org/short-reads/2025/03/05/what-the-data-says-about-gun-deaths-in-the-us/.

28 '"No Way to Prevent This", Says Only Nation Where This Regularly Happens', *The Onion*, 27 May 2014.

29 The quotation is often wrongly attributed to French prime minister Georges Clemenceau, among others. In fact, it was *La Liberté* objecting to the First World War debt-repayment policies of the Hoover administration. It was translated from the French, appearing in 'Herriot Admits Pact Not Aimed at Debt to U.S.', *Washington Post*, 16 July 1932, p. 1.

30 Robert Pinsky, *Democracy, Culture and the Voice of Poetry* (Princeton, NJ: Princeton University Press, 2005), p. 76.

31 Lawrence W. Levine, 'Jazz and American Culture', *The Journal of American Folklore*, vol. 102, no. 403, January–March 1989, p. 6.

32 Gary Shteyngart, 'My Parents Got Me Out of Soviet Russia at the Right Time. Should My Family Now Leave the US?', *Guardian*, 17 July 2025, https://www.theguardian.com/books/2025/jul/19/my-parents-got-me-out-of-soviet-russia-at-the-right-time-should-my-family-now-leave-the-us.

33 Vivian C. Sobchack, 'Beyond Visual Aids: American Film as American Culture', *American Quarterly*, vol. 32, no. 3, 1980, p. 280.

34 Howard Palmer, 'Mosaic Versus Melting Pot? Immigration and Ethnicity in Canada and the United States', *International Journal*, vol. 31, no. 3, Summer 1976, p. 488.

35 Charles Hirschman, 'The Contributions of Immigrants to American Culture', *Daedalus*, vol. 142, no. 3, Summer 2013, p. 6.

36 US Department of Homeland Security, Office of Homeland Security Statistics, 'Table 39. Aliens Removed or Returned: Fiscal Years 1892 to 2015', https://ohss.dhs.gov/topics/immigration/yearbook/2015/table39.

37 Philip Roth, 'Writing American Fiction', *Commentary*, March 1961.

38 John Adams assessed that one-third of Americans supported the revolution, one-third opposed and one-third were neutral. Contemporary historians tracking the 60,000–80,000 Loyalists who fled during and after the revolution are more inclined to put the proportion of opponents at about 20%. See George Washington Presidential Library, 'Loyalists', https://www.mountvernon.org/library/digitalhistory/digital-encyclopedia/article/loyalists.

39 Federalist No. 51 is claimed by both Alexander Hamilton and James Madison. See 'The Federalist No. 51', Founders Online, US National Archives and Records Administration, 6 February 1788, https://founders.archives.gov/documents/Hamilton/01-04-02-0199. See also Roger H. Davidson, '"Invitation to Struggle": An Overview of Legislative–Executive Relations', *The Annals of the American Academy of Political and Social Science*, vol. 499, no. 1, September 1988.

40 Alexis de Tocqueville, *Democracy in America*, Chapter XVI: Causes Mitigating Tyranny in The United States, Part I, https://americanliterature.com/author/alexis-de-tocqueville/book/democracy-in-america/chapter-xvi-causes-mitigating-tyranny-in-the-united-states-part-i.

41 James Madison, writing as Publius, 'The Federalist Number 10', Founders Online, US National Archives and Records Administration, 22 November 1787, https://founders.archives.gov/documents/Madison/01-10-02-0178.

42 Polybius, *The Histories*: Book III, chapter 2, section 167 (London: Macmillan, 1889), https://www.gutenberg.org/files/44125/44125-h/44125-h.htm.

43 E.E. Schattschneider, quoted in Sean Trende, 'A Referendum on the President', RealClear Politics, 5 November 2014, https://www.realclearpolitics.com/articles/2014/11/05/a_referendum_on_the_president_124577.html.

44 Molly Worthen, *Spellbound: How Charisma Shaped American History from the Puritans to Donald Trump* (London: Random House, 2025), pp. xviii–xix.

45 Lincoln's point was that the Confederacy would succeed at secession if the Union failed to hold the border states electorally. Abraham Lincoln, quoted in 'Abraham Lincoln and Emancipation', Library of Congress Abraham Lincoln Papers, https://www.loc.gov/collections/abraham-lincoln-papers/articles-and-essays/abraham-lincoln-and-emancipation/.

46 Timothy P. Carney, *Alienated America: Why Some Places Thrive While Others Collapse* (London: HarperCollins, 2019), p. 90.

47 Cara Korte, 'What the U.S. Is Committing to as It Rejoins the Paris Climate Accords – And Why It Matters', CBS News, 19 February 2021, https://www.cbsnews.com/news/paris-agreement-united-states-commitment/; and Caroline Weiss, 'America and the Paris Agreement: Withdrawal, Recommitment, and Future Implications', Climate and Global Change Center, University of Pittsburgh, 17 March 2021, https://www.climatecenter.pitt.edu/news/america-and-paris-agreement-withdrawal-recommitment-and-future-implications.

48 Luis Andres Henao, 'US Catholic Bishops Decry Trump's Immigration Raids Upending Church Life', Associated Press, 12 September 2025, https://apnews.com/article/immigration-raids-catholic-bishops-church-trump-d3f8edcaa771180d630196e49d4841a2.

49 Jeanne Bonner, 'New York May Have America's Top Pizza, but LA Is at Its Heels, Italian Judges Say', CNN, 3 July 2025; and J. Kenji López-Alt, 'Detroit Style Pan Pizza', Serious Eats, January 2025, https://www.seriouseats.com/detroit-style-pizza-recipe.

50 Josh Moody, 'A Guide to the Changing Number of U.S. Universities', U.S. News and World Report, 27 April 2021, https://www.usnews.com/education/best-colleges/articles/how-many-universities-are-in-the-us-and-why-that-number-is-changing.

51 'World University Rankings 2026', *Times Higher Education*, https://www.timeshighereducation.com/world-university-rankings/latest/world-ranking.

52 World Population Review, 'Arable Land by Country 2025', https://worldpopulationreview.com/country-rankings/arable-land-by-country.

53 Sean Ross, '4 Countries That Produce the Most Food', Investopedia, 4 April 2025, https://www.investopedia.com/articles/investing/100615/4-countries-produce-most-food.asp.

54 Hannah Ritchie, Pablo Rosado and Max Roser, 'Energy Production and Consumption', Our World in Data, 2024, https://ourworldindata.org/energy-production-consumption.

55 Abigail Tierney, 'Exports of Goods and Services from the United States from 1990 to 2023, as a Percentage of Gross Domestic Product', Statista, 7 January 2025, https://www.statista.com/statistics/258779/us-exports-as-a-percentage-of-gdp/.

56 Robert O. Keohane and Joseph S. Nye, Jr., 'The End of the Long American Century: Trump and the Sources of U.S. Power', *Foreign Affairs*, July/August 2025, https://www.foreignaffairs.com/united-states/end-long-american-century-trump-keohane-nye.

57 Adam Tooze, 'Is a Decade of American Exceptionalism Coming to an End?', Chartbook, 16 July 2025, https://adamtooze.substack.com/p/is-a-decade-of-american-exceptionalism.

58 *Ibid.*

59 Sebastian Mallaby, *The Power Law: Venture Capital and the Making of the New Future* (London: Penguin, 2022), p. 11.

60 Conor Moore and Francois Chadwick, '2024 Global VC Investment Rises to $368 Billion as Investor Interest in AI Soars, While IPO Optimism Grows for 2025 According to KPMG Private Enterprise's Venture Pulse', KPMG, https://kpmg.com/xx/en/media/press-releases/2025/01/2024-global-vc-investment-rises-to-368-billion-dollars.html.

61 Stuart C. Gilson, quoted in Kim Girard, 'How Chapter 11 Saved the U.S. Economy', Harvard Business School, 25 March 2013, https://www.library.hbs.edu/working-knowledge/how-chapter-11-saved-the-us-economy.

62 Tom Fairless and David Luhnow, 'The Tech Industry Is Huge – and Europe's Share of It Is Very Small', *Wall Street Journal*, 19 May 2025, https://www.wsj.com/tech/europe-big-tech-ai-1f3f862c.

63 Theodore Roosevelt, quoted in Shane Reiner-Roth, 'West of West Finds Opportunity for Social Interaction in Places with Little Supply', *The Architect's Newspaper*, 17 October 2023, https://www.archpaper.com/2023/10/west-of-west-opportunity-social-interaction-places-little-supply/.

64 Henry Farrell and Abraham L. Newman, 'The Enshittification of American Power', WIRED, 15 July 2025, https://www.wired.com/story/enshittification-of-american-power/.

65 Dan Williams, 'Scapegoating the Algorithm', Asterisk, July 2025, https://asteriskmag.com/issues/11/scapegoating-the-algorithm.

66 'The Economics of Superintelligence', *The Economist*, 24 July 2025, https://www.economist.com/leaders/2025/07/24/the-economics-of-superintelligence.

67 Mallaby, *The Power Law*, p. 12.

68 World Population Review, 'Immigration by Country 2025', https://worldpopulationreview.com/country-rankings/immigration-by-country.

69 Steven A. Camarota and Karen Zeigler, 'The Declining Education Level of Newly Arrived Immigrants', Center for Immigration Studies, 19 February 2025, https://cis.org/Report/Declining-Education-Level-Newly-Arrived-Immigrants.

70 Peter Dizikes, 'Study: Immigrants in the US Are More Likely to Start Firms, Create Jobs', MIT News, 9 May 2022, https://news.mit.edu/2022/study-immigrants-more-likely-start-firms-create-jobs-0509.

71 Pierre Azoulay et al., 'Immigration and Entrepreneurship in the United States', *American Economic Review: Insights*, vol. 4, no. 1, March 2022.

72 Stephen Nickell, 'Is the U.S. Labor Market Really That Exceptional? A Review of Richard Freeman's "America Works: The Exceptional U.S. Labor Market"', *Journal of Economic Literature*, vol. 46, no. 2, June 2008, pp. 384–5.

73 Michael R. Strain, *The American Dream Is Not Dead (But Populism Could Kill It)* (West Conshohocken, PA: Templeton Press, 2020), p. 28.

74 Fairless and Luhnow, 'The Tech Industry Is Huge – and Europe's Share of It Is Very Small'.

75 Italian entrepreneur Fabrizio Capobianco, quoted in Fairless and Luhnow, 'The Tech Industry Is Huge – and Europe's Share of It Is Very Small'.

76 Martin Wolf, 'Trump's Assault on the Global Dollar', *Financial Times*, 20 May 2025, https://www.ft.com/

content/d9656820-0b3e-46e7-97c9-b6684d558776.

77 'What Is the Richest Country in the World in 2025?', *The Economist*, 18 July 2025, https://www.economist.com/graphic-detail/2025/07/18/what-is-the-richest-country-in-the-world-in-2025.

78 Official Chinese economic data is likely exaggerated, perhaps by up to 30%. See Derek Scissors, 'US–China: Who Is Bigger and When?', American Enterprise Institute, 26 March 2019, https://www.aei.org/research-products/report/us-china-who-is-bigger-and-when/.

79 Fairless and Luhnow, 'The Tech Industry Is Huge – and Europe's Share of It Is Very Small'.

80 Bafundi Maronoti, 'Revisiting the International Role of the Dollar', *Bank for International Settlements Quarterly Review*, 5 December 2022, https://www.bis.org/publ/qtrpdf/r_qt2212x.htm.

81 Toby Nangle, 'Understanding the Methodology Behind Moody's US Downgrade', *Financial Times*, 20 May 2025, https://www.ft.com/content/44fdf19d-cfdd-443a-99d3-841993f46ebe.

82 Wolf, 'Trump's Assault on the Global Dollar'.

83 Michael Pettis, 'A (Very Short) History of Global Reserve Currencies', *Financial Times*, 7 June 2023, https://www.ft.com/content/c967ba48-f21b-4222-9f11-beb61ce710ae.

84 *Ibid*.

85 According to Eaglen's calculations, China's defence budget reached the equivalent of US$711bn in recent years – more than three times the official figure. See Mackenzie Eaglen, 'Keeping Up with the Pacing Threat: Unveiling the True Size of Beijing's Military Spending', American Enterprise Institute, 29 April 2024, https://www.aei.org/research-products/report/keeping-up-with-the-pacing-threat-unveiling-the-true-size-of-beijings-military-spending/; and Fenella McGerty and Karl Dewey, 'Interactive: Global Defence Spending in 2024', IISS, 13 February 2025, https://www.iiss.org/publications/the-military-balance/2025/interactive-global-defence-spending-in-2024/.

86 Collin Meisel, Jonathan D. Moyer and Sarah Gutberlet, 'How Do You Actually Measure Military Capability?', Modern War Institute at West Point, 1 September 2020, https://mwi.westpoint.edu/how-do-you-actually-measure-military-capability/.

87 US Department of Defense, Defense Casualty Analysis System, 'U.S. Active Duty Military Deaths by Year and Manner', August 2023, https://dcas.dmdc.osd.mil/dcas/app/summaryData/deaths/byYearManner.

88 @rickywlmsbong on the social-media platform Bluesky, quoted in Kori Schake, 'Don't Rain on the Soldiers' Parade', The Dispatch, 17 June 2025, https://thedispatch.com/article/trump-parade-army-march-patriotism/.

89 John E. Wissler, 'Logistics: The Lifeblood of Military Power', Heritage Foundation, 4 October 2018, https://www.heritage.org/military-strength-topical-essays/2019-essays/logistics-the-lifeblood-military-power.

90 US Department of Defense, 'Austin, Milley Say DOD Laser-focused on Kabul Evacuation Mission', 18 August 2021, https://www.defense.gov/Explore/News/Article/Article/2737183/austin-milley-say-dod-laser-focused-on-kabul-evacuation-mission/.

91 Mohamed Younis, 'Confidence in US Military Lowest in Over Two Decades', Gallup News, 31 July 2023, https://news.gallup.com/poll/509189/confidence-military-lowest-two-decades.aspx.

92 Ben Watson, 'Mapped: America's Collective Defense Agreements', Defense One, 3 February 2017, https://

www.defenseone.com/ideas/2017/02/mapped-americas-collective-defense-agreements/135114/; 'Where Are U.S. Troops Stationed?', USAFacts, https://usafacts.org/articles/where-are-us-military-members-stationed-and-why/; Theodore McLauchlin, Lee J.M. Seymour and Simon Pierre Boulanger Martel, 'Tracking the Rise of United States Foreign Military Training, IMTAD-USA, a New Dataset and Research Agenda', National Library of Medicine, 20 February 2022, https://pmc.ncbi.nlm.nih.gov/articles/PMC8969074/; and 'US Arms Exports in 2023 by Country', Statista, https://www.statista.com/statistics/248552/us-arms-exports-by-country/.

93 Ben Barry et al., 'Defending Europe Without the United States: Costs and Consequences', IISS, May 2025, p. 4, https://www.iiss.org/research-paper/2025/05/defending-europe-without--the-united-states-costs-and-consequences/.

94 World Bank, 'Military Expenditure (% of GDP)', https://data.worldbank.org/indicator/MS.MIL.XPND.GD.ZS.

95 Paul Kennedy, *The Rise and Fall of the Great Powers* (London: Vintage Books, 1989), p. 514.

96 James Fallows, 'How America Can Rise Again', *Atlantic*, January/February 2010, https://www.theatlantic.com/magazine/archive/2010/01/how-america-can-rise-again/307839/.

97 Saclan Bercovitch, *The American Jeremiad* (Madison, WI: University of Wisconsin Press, 1978).

98 'Ten Indicators of What's Going On with America's Economy', *The Economist*, 2 August 2025, https://www.economist.com/graphic-detail/2025/03/14/ten-indicators-of-whats-going-on-with-americas-economy.

99 'How to Win at Foreign Policy', *The Economist*, 14 August 2025, https://www.economist.com/leaders/2025/08/14/how-to-win-at-foreign-policy; and 'How Is Trump's Brazil-bashing Putting America First?', *The Economist*, 7 August 2025, https://www.economist.com/united-states/2025/08/07/how-is-trumps-brazil-bashing-putting-america-first.

100 Adam Posen, 'The New Economic Geography', *Foreign Affairs*, 19 August 2025, https://www.foreignaffairs.com/united-states/new-economic-geography-posen.

101 William J. Burns, 'A Letter to America's Discarded Public Servants', *Atlantic*, 20 August 2025, https://www.theatlantic.com/magazine/archive/2025/10/trump-retribution-public-servants/683914/.

102 Michael Johnston, 'The New American Hustle', *Foreign Affairs*, 6 August 2025, https://www.foreignaffairs.com/united-states/new-american-hustle.

103 K. Oanh Ha, 'Student Arrivals to US Continue to Plummet, with Asia Hit Especially Hard', Bloomberg, 18 August 2025, https://www.bloomberg.com/news/articles/2025-08-19/student-arrivals-to-us-plummet-for-fourth-month-asia-hit-hard?embedded-checkout=true.

104 Posen, 'The New Economic Geography'.

105 'Ten Indicators of What's Going on with America's Economy'; and 'US EPU (Monthly, Daily, Categorical)', Economic Policy Uncertainty, https://www.policyuncertainty.com/us_monthly.html.

106 Greg Ip, 'The U.S. Marches Toward State Capitalism with American Characteristics', *Wall Street Journal*, 11 August 2025, https://www.wsj.com/economy/the-u-s-marches-toward-state-capitalism-with-american-characteristics-f75cafa8?msockid=1580af722ac46e523066b9032bd16f5f.

107 'Monetary Policy and the Fed's Framework Review', speech

delivered by Jerome H. Powell, Chair of the Federal Reserve, Jackson Hole (WY), 21 August 2025, https://www.federalreserve.gov/newsevents/speech/powell20250822a.htm.

[108] Powell also expressed hope that the effects of tariffs would be 'relatively short-lived'. See US Federal Reserve, 'Transcript of Chair Powell's Press Conference Opening Statement', 10 December 2025, https://www.federalreserve.gov/mediacenter/files/FOMCpresconf20251210.pdf.

[109] Michael D. Swaine, 'Chinese Views of U.S. Decline', China Leadership Monitor, 1 September 2021, https://www.prcleader.org/post/chinese-views-of-u-s-decline.

[110] Timothy R. Heath, 'Why Is China Strengthening Its Military? It's Not All About War', RAND, 24 March 2023, https://www.rand.org/pubs/commentary/2023/03/why-is-china-strengthening-its-military-its-not-all.html; and Admiral Sam Paparo, quoted in David Vergun, 'China's Military Buildup Threatens Indo-Pacific Region Security', DOD News, 9 April 2025, https://www.war.gov/News/News-Stories/Article/Article/4150802/chinas-military-buildup-threatens-indo-pacific-region-security/.

[111] China and US ship numbers are from IISS analysis based on Military Balance+ data on Chinese and US holdings of major warships (major submarines; aircraft carriers and other principal surface combatants including cruisers, destroyers and frigates; corvettes and patrol ships; principal amphibious ships and landing ships; and mine warfare vessels). For shipbuilding capacity, see Brandon J. Weichert, 'China's Shipbuilding Capacity: 232 Times Greater than United States', The National Interest, 13 September 2024, https://nationalinterest.org/blog/buzz/chinas-shipbuilding-capacity-232-times-greater-united-states-212736.

[112] Andrew S. Erickson, 'PRC Pursuit of Xi's 2027 "Centennial Military Building Goal" (建军一百年奋斗目标): Sources & Analysis', 18 April 2023, https://www.andrewerickson.com/2021/12/prc-pursuit-of-2027-centennial-military-building-goal-sources-analysis/.

[113] Donald Trump, quoted in Didi Tang, 'Trump Says Taiwan Should Pay More for Defense and Dodges Questions If He Would Defend the Island', Associated Press, 7 July 2024, https://apnews.com/article/trump-taiwan-chips-invasion-china-910e7a94b19248fc75e5d1ab6b0a34d8; Donald Trump, quoted in 'Trump's Unification Remark Raises Eyebrows in Taiwan', China Academy, 14 May 2025, https://thechinaacademy.org/trumps-unification-remark-sparks-uproar-in-taiwan/; and Elbridge Colby, quoted in Alexander Bolton, 'GOP Senators Grill Trump Defense Nominee on Iran, Taiwan, NATO', Hill, 4 March 2025, https://thehill.com/homenews/senate/5175389-gop-senators-elbridge-colby-confirmation-hearing/.

[114] Thomas Wright, 'Trump's 19th Century Foreign Policy', Politico, 20 January 2016, https://www.politico.com/magazine/story/2016/01/donald-trump-foreign-policy-213546/.

[115] Jack Detsch et al., 'Trump Allies Caught Off Guard by Pentagon's Ukraine Weapons Freeze', Politico, 3 July 2023, https://www.politico.com/news/2025/07/02/ukraine-weapons-freeze-elbridge-colby-00438156.

[116] Kevin Liptak et al., 'Trump and Vance Erupt at Zelensky in Tense Oval Office Meeting', CNN, 28 February 2025, https://edition.cnn.com/2025/02/28/politics/trump-zelensky-vance-oval-office; Jeffrey Goldberg, 'The Trump Administration Accidentally Texted Me Their Warplans', Atlantic, 26

March 2025, https://www.theatlantic.com/politics/archive/2025/03/trump-administration-accidentally-texted-me-its-war-plans/682151/; 'A Week That Felt Like a Decade: Europe Reels from J.D. Vance's Speech in Munich', European University Institute, 27 February 2025, https://www.eui.eu/news-hub?id=a-week-that-felt-like-a-decade-europe-reels-from-j.d.-vances-speech-in-munich; Allan Smith and Carol E. Lee, 'Pressure on China and Pure "Trolling": Why Trump Is Pushing an Expansionist Agenda', NBC News, 9 January 2025, https://www.yahoo.com/news/pressure-china-pure-trolling-why-182900486.html; and 'National Security Strategy of the United States of America', November 2025, https://www.whitehouse.gov/wp-content/uploads/2025/12/2025-National-Security-Strategy.pdf.

117 Mark Sappenfield, 'Why Europe's Trade Deal with the US Might Be Better than It Seems', *Christian Science Monitor*, 29 July 2025, https://www.csmonitor.com/World/Europe/2025/0729/trump-eu-trade-deal-tariff-europe.

118 He also added that he was 'committed to being their friends'. Donald Trump, quoted in 'Trump Says Commitment to NATO Mutual Defense Guarantee "Depends on Your Definition"', PBS, 25 June 2025, https://www.pbs.org/newshour/world/trump-says-commitment-to-nato-mutual-defense-guarantee-depends-on-your-definition.

119 Brett Samuels, 'Trump on NATO Mutual Defense Clause: "If I Didn't Stand With It, I Wouldn't Be Here"', *Hill*, 25 June 2025, https://thehill.com/homenews/administration/5368418-trump-nato-article-5-support/.

120 Donald Trump, quoted in Joseph Ataman and Clare Sebastian, 'Inside the NATO Charm Offensive that Shocked as Much as It Delivered',

CNN, 26 June 2025, https://edition.cnn.com/2025/06/25/europe/rutte-daddy-trump-nato-ukraine-intl-latam.

121 Ali Mammadov, 'If America Abandons Europe, Will the Continent Fragment or Unify?', War on the Rocks, 12 June 2025, https://warontherocks.com/2025/06/if-america-abandons-europe-will-the-continent-fragment-or-unify/.

122 Paweł Skrzypczyński, cited in Menzie Chinn, 'A Quasi-real Time Measure of the Average Effective Tariff Rate', Econbrowser, 29 July 2025, https://econbrowser.com/archives/2025/07/a-quasi-real-time-measure-of-the-average-effective-tariff-rate.

123 Canadian Prime Minister Mark Carney, quoted in Farrell and Newman, 'The Enshittification of American Power'.

124 G. John Ikenberry, 'Institutions, Strategic Restraint, and the Persistence of American Postwar Order', *International Security*, vol. 23, no. 3, Winter 1988–89, p. 44. The term 'liberal leviathan' is used in Ikenberry's later work *Liberal Leviathan: The Origins, Crisis, and Transformation of the American World Order* (Princeton, NJ: Princeton University Press, 2011).

125 Ikenberry, 'Institutions, Strategic Restraint, and the Persistence of American Postwar Order', p. 45.

126 *Ibid.*

127 'Trump Wants to Command Bosses Like Xi Does. He Is Failing', *The Economist*, 13 August 2025, https://www.economist.com/business/2025/08/13/trump-wants-to-command-bosses-like-xi-does-he-is-failing.

128 Yuval Noah Harari, 'Trump's World of Rival Fortresses', *Financial Times*, 18 April 2025, https://www.ft.com/content/06cc7b0f-3e32-4164-b096-ff92a1532236.

129 Thucydides, *The History of the Peloponnesian Wars*, Book 5.89, https://

www.gutenberg.org/files/7142/7142-h/7142-h.htm#link2H_4_0019.

130 Nancy A. Youssef, Jonathan Lemire and Missy Ryan, 'The Pentagon's Policy Guy Is All In on China', *Atlantic*, 28 July 2025, https://www.theatlantic.com/national-security/archive/2025/07/pentagon-china-elbridge-colby/683677/.

131 Interview with Ursula von der Leyen, 'We Have No Bros and No Oligarchs', *Die Zeit*, 15 April 2025, https://www.zeit.de/politik/2025-04/ursula-von-der-leyen-eu-usa-donald-trump-english.

132 Ulrich Laderner and Bernd Ulrich in interview with Ursula von der Leyen, 'We Have No Bros and No Oligarchs'.

133 Ruchir Sharma, 'The World Is Moving On to Trade Without the US', *Financial Times*, 26 January 2025, https://www.ft.com/content/07eac548-6607-4c88-bfe3-4f1d6e3b8cf2.

134 Kori Schake, 'Dispensable Nation: America in a Post-American World', *Foreign Affairs*, July/August 2025, https://www.foreignaffairs.com/united-states/dispensable-nation-schake.

135 'What Economics Can Teach Foreign-policy Types', *The Economist*, 24 July 2025, https://www.economist.com/finance-and-economics/2025/07/24/what-economics-can-teach-foreign-policy-types.

136 Fallows, 'How America Can Rise Again'.

137 'Chinese Media Breaks Silence on "Unprecedented Chaos" of US Vote', Bloomberg, 5 November 2025, https://www.bloomberg.com/news/articles/2024-11-05/chinese-media-breaks-silence-on-unprecedented-chaos-of-us-vote.

138 H.L. Mencken, quoted in Henry I. Miller, 'No Politician Left Behind', Hoover Institution, 22 September 2011, https://www.hoover.org/research/no-politician-left-behind.

139 Mark Twain, *Pudd'nhead Wilson's New Calendar*, cited in Mark Twain, *Following the Equator*, Chapter 8, 1897, https://www.online-literature.com/twain/following-the-equator/8/.

140 Neil Postman, cited in Ryan Zickgraf, 'The World Is Choking on Screens. Just as This Book Foretold: Neil Postman's "Amusing Ourselves to Death" at 40 Is Truer than Ever', *Washington Post*, 17 July 2025, https://www.washingtonpost.com/opinions/2025/07/17/neil-postman-amusing-ourselves-to-death/.

141 Yuval Levin, 'What's Wrong with Congress (and How to Fix It)', *Atlantic*, 11 June 2024, https://www.theatlantic.com/ideas/archive/2024/06/congress-reform-filibuster-constitution/678604/.

142 Jaclyn Diaz, 'What Happens if Trump Starts Ignoring Court Rulings? We Break It Down', National Public Radio, 12 February 2025, https://www.npr.org/2025/02/12/nx-s1-5293132/trump-vance-constitutional-crisis-court-rulings. On Trump's felony conviction, see Peter Charalambous and Ivan Pereira, 'Donald Trump Becomes 1st US President Tried and Convicted of Crimes', ABC News, 31 May 2024, https://abcnews.go.com/US/former-president-donald-trump-found-guilty-manhattan-hush/story?id=110647273.

143 Megan Brenan, 'Independents Drive Trump's Approval to 37% Second-term Low', Gallup News, 24 July 2025, https://news.gallup.com/poll/692879/independents-drive-trump-approval-second-term-low.aspx.

144 Strain, *The American Dream Is Not Dead*, p. 63.

145 Nicholas Eberstadt, *Men Without Work: America's Invisible Crisis* (West Conshohocken, PA: Templeton Press, 2016).

146 IMF, World Economic Outlook Update, 'Global Economy: Tenuous Resilience amid Persistent Uncertainty', July 2025, https://

www.imf.org/en/Publications/WEO/
Issues/2025/07/29/world-economic-
outlook-update-july-2025.

147 Natasha Piñon, 'More Companies
than "Normal" Are Withdrawing
Guidance for the Quarter as
Uncertainty About Tariffs Looms,
UBS Analyst Says', *Fortune*, 19 March
2025, https://fortune.com/article/
more-companies-than-normal-
withdrawing-guidance-ubs-analyst/.

148 Trading Economics, '10-year Bond
Yields', https://tradingeconomics.
com/bonds.

149 Elizabeth Crisp, 'Trump Trying
to Make Powell "as Miserable as
Possible": Haberman', *Hill*, 11 July
2025, https://thehill.com/homenews/
administration/5396460-trump-
powell-fed-rift/.

150 Justin Baer, 'JPMorgan's Jamie
Dimon Predicts "Crack in the Bond
Market", Citing U.S. Fiscal Mess',
Wall Street Journal, 30 May 2025,
https://www.wsj.com/finance/
jpmorgans-jamie-dimon-predicts-
crack-in-the-bond-market-citing-u-s-
fiscal-mess-9d90cb3f.

151 Patricio Martín, 'US Dollar Loses
Interest After Weak Retail Sales
Figures', FXStreet, 14 February
2025, https://www.fxstreet.com/
news/us-dollar-extends-losses-
as-weak-retail-sales-weigh-on-
sentiment-202502141805.

152 'Has Trump Damaged the Dollar?',
The Economist, 20 July 2025, https://
www.economist.com/finance-
and-economics/2025/07/20/
has-trump-damaged-the-dollar.

153 'The Dollar's Sell-off Raises Concerns
that Investors Are Losing Trust in
the U.S.', CBS News, 18 April 2025,
https://www.cbsnews.com/news/
us-dollar-value-decline-trump-sell-
off-tariffs/.

154 'Has Trump Damaged the Dollar?'.

155 Adam Tooze, 'Chartbook 401:
The Dollar System in an Age
of Market-based Finance –

Financial Globalization Beyond
Banks', 30 July 2025, https://
adamtooze.substack.com/p/
chartbook-401-the-dollar-system-in.

156 Bank for International Settlements,
'Annual Economic Report', July
2025, p. 26, https://www.bis.org/
annualeconomicreports/index.htm.

157 'The Dollar's Sell-off Raises
Concerns that Investors Are Losing
Trust in the U.S.'.

158 Huileng Tang, 'China and Russia
Are Working on Homegrown
Alternatives to the SWIFT Payment
System. Here's What They Would
Mean for the US Dollar', Business
Insider, 28 April 2022, https://www.
businessinsider.com/china-russia-
alternative-swift-payment-cips-spfs-
yuan-ruble-dollar-2022-4.

159 Jeanna Smialek, 'America's Allies
Want to Redraw the World's Trade
Map, Minus the U.S.', *Seattle Times*, 13
July 2025, https://www.seattletimes.
com/business/american-allies-want-
to-redraw-the-worlds-trade-map-
minus-the-u-s/.

160 Jeanna Smialek and Matina Stevens-
Gridneff, 'Canada and EU Pull
Together as America Pushes Them
Away', *New York Times*, 23 June 2025,
https://www.nytimes.com/2025/06/23/
world/europe/canada-eu-security-
defense-trump.html; and Jeanna
Smialek, 'E.U. and U.K. Strike a Deal:
What to Know', *New York Times*, 19
May 2025, https://www.nytimes.
com/2025/05/19/world/europe/uk-eu-
summit-starmer.html.

161 'South Korea, China, Japan Agree to
Promote Regional Trade as Trump
Tariffs Loom', Reuters, 30 March
2025, https://www.reuters.com/
world/asia-pacific/south-korea-china-
japan-agree-promote-regional-trade-
trump-tariffs-loom-2025-03-30/.

162 Nicholas Grossman, 'Trump's Trade
Policies Threaten to Strengthen
China, Not Weaken It', MSNBC,
17 April 2025, https://www.msnbc.

com/opinion/msnbc-opinion/trump-global-trade-china-america-first-rcna201647.

163 Andreas Bauer, quoted in Sappenfield, 'Why Europe's Trade Deal with the US Might Be Better than It Seems'.

164 Ross Andersen, 'Every Scientific Empire Comes to an End', *Atlantic*, 31 July 2025, https://www.theatlantic.com/science/archive/2025/07/science-empire-america-decline/683711/.

165 'Who Is Ahead in the Global Tech Race?', *The Economist*, 6 June 2025, https://www.economist.com/graphic-detail/2025/06/06/who-is-ahead-in-the-global-tech-race.

166 Jennifer Wong Leung, Stephan Robin and Danielle Cave, 'ASPI's Two-decade Critical Technology Tracker: The Rewards of Long-term Research Investment', Australian Strategic Policy Institute, 28 August 2024, https://www.aspi.org.au/report/aspis-two-decade-critical-technology-tracker/.

167 David Autor and Gordon Hanson, 'We Warned About the First China Shock. The Next One Will Be Worse', *New York Times*, 14 July 2025, https://www.nytimes.com/2025/07/14/opinion/china-shock-economy-manufacturing.html.

168 Kyle Chan, 'In the Future, China Will Be Dominant. The U.S. Will Be Irrelevant', *New York Times*, 19 May 2025, https://www.nytimes.com/2025/05/19/opinion/china-us-trade-tariffs.html.

169 Farrell and Newman, 'The Enshittification of American Power'.

170 White House, 'President Trump Is Leading with Peace Through Strength', 4 March 2025, https://www.whitehouse.gov/articles/2025/03/president-trump-is-leading-with-peace-through-strength/.

171 *Ibid*.

172 The calculation was done by my AEI colleague, Todd Harrison, cited with permission.

173 Todd Harrison, 'Is Trump's Golden Dome a Brilliant Idea or a Gilded Boondoggle?', American Enterprise Institute, 8 April 2025, https://www.aei.org/articles/is-trumps-golden-dome-a-brilliant-idea-or-a-gilded-boondoggle/.

174 Claus Hjort Frederiksen, quoted in Yaroslav Trofiimov, 'Trump's Fixation with Greenland Has Ended Denmark's Love Affair with the U.S.', *Wall Street Journal*, 22 July 2025, https://www.wsj.com/world/europe/trump-denmark-relationship-greenland-489239ff?msockid=31f6369af4266dc133f22008f5376cc1.

175 Csongor Körömi, 'Majority of Europeans See Trump as an Enemy, Survey Shows', Politico, 20 March 2025, https://www.politico.eu/article/half-europeans-see-donald-trump-as-enemy/.

176 Schake, 'Dispensable Nation: America in a Post-American World'.

177 Friedrich Merz, quoted in Tim Ross and Nette Nöstlinger, 'Germany's Merz Vows "Independence" from Trump's America, Warning NATO May Soon Be Dead', Politico, 23 February 2025, https://www.politico.eu/article/friedrich-merz-germany-election-united-states-donald-trump-nato/.

178 Lawrence Freedman, 'A New Nuclear Role for Britain and France', Comment Is Freed, 13 July 2025, https://samf.substack.com/p/a-new-nuclear-role-for-britain-and.

179 'The EU Wants to Break Its Security Dependency on the US and Buy More European Weapons', Associated Press, 19 March 2025, https://apnews.com/article/eu-defense-us-ukraine-industry-ammunition-weapons-ea03077814f9113b548d7281f32a11b5.

180 Kori Schake, *The State and the Soldier: A History of Civil–Military Relations in the United States* (Cambridge: Polity, 2025), pp. 140–1.

181 Fallows, 'How America Can Rise Again'.

182 Giovanna Coi, 'US Popularity Collapses Worldwide in Wake of Trump's Return', Politico, 12 May 2025, https://www.politico.eu/article/usa-popularity-collapse-worldwide-trump-return/.

183 Dee-Ann Durbin, 'US Expected a Big Travel Year, but Overseas Visitors – Angered by Trump – Are Heading Elsewhere', AP News, 8 April 2025, https://apnews.com/article/tourism-us-travel-trump-visitors-international-14c31b490fd382d09ad5cae625ddc937.

184 Greg Iacurci, 'Fewer International Tourists Are Visiting the U.S – Economic Losses Could Be "Staggering," Researchers Estimate', CNBC, 28 May 2025, https://www.cnbc.com/2025/05/28/travel-spending-us-from-overseas-tourists-to-fall-in-2025.html.

185 Ibid.

186 Rebecca Jacobs, 'Trump's Term 2 Corruption By the Numbers: More Golf Trips, More Foreign Visitors and More Profits', Citizens for Responsibility and Ethics in Washington, 21 July 2025, https://www.citizensforethics.org/reports-investigations/crew-reports/trumps-term-2-corruption-by-the-numbers-more-golf-trips-more-foreign-visitors-and-more-profits/; Isaac Chotiner, 'Donald Trump's Culture of Corruption', New Yorker, 16 May 2025, https://www.newyorker.com/news/q-and-a/donald-trumps-culture-of-corruption; David Frum, 'The Trump Presidency's World-historical Heist', Atlantic, 28 May 2025, https://www.theatlantic.com/ideas/archive/2025/05/trump-golden-age-corruption/682935/; Peter Baker, 'As Trumps Monetize Presidency, Profits Outstrip Protests', New York Times, 25 May 2025, https://www.nytimes.com/2025/05/25/us/politics/trump-money-plane-crypto.html; Patricia Clarke, 'How the US President and His Clan Ushered In a New Golden Age of Corruption', Observer, 11 May 2025, https://observer.co.uk/news/international/article/trump-inc-family-corruption; Tom Burgis, 'All the President's Millions: How the Trumps Are Turning the Presidency into Riches', Guardian, 30 November 2025, https://www.theguardian.com/us-news/ng-interactive/2025/nov/30/all-the-presidents-millions-how-the-trumps-are-turning-the-presidency-into-riches; and Casey Michel, 'America Has Never Seen Corruption Like This', Atlantic, 10 July 2025, https://www.theatlantic.com/politics/archive/2025/07/trump-corruption-foreign-regimes/683487/.

187 Keohane and Nye, Jr., 'The End of the Long American Century'.

188 Shteyngart, 'My Parents Got Me Out of Soviet Russia at the Right Time. Should My Family Now Leave the US?'.

189 Stefan Rebenich, 'Late Antiquity in Modern Eyes', in Philip Rousseau (ed.), A Companion to Late Antiquity (Malden, MA: John Wiley and Sons, 2009), p. 78.

190 Camilla Townsend, Fifth Sun: A New History of the Aztecs (Oxford: Oxford University Press, 2019), p. 10.

191 Frederick W. Mote, Imperial China, 900–1800 (Cambridge, MA: Harvard University Press, 2003), pp. 835, 849.

192 Schake, Safe Passage, p. 1.

193 Michael A. Reynolds, Shattering Empires: The Clash and Collapse of the Ottoman and Russian Empires 1908–1918 (Cambridge: Cambridge University Press, 2011), p. 324.

194 David Webster, 'The Classic Maya Collapse', in Deborah L. Nichols (ed.), The Oxford Handbook of Mesoamerican Archaeology (Oxford: Oxford University Press, 2016), p. 324.

195 S.C. Gwynne, Empire of the Summer Moon: Quanah Parker and the Rise and Fall of the Comanches (New York: Scribner, 2011), pp. 1–2.

196 Webster, 'The Classic Maya Collapse'.

197 Sergey Radchenko, *To Run the World: The Kremlin's Cold War Bid for Global Power* (Cambridge: Cambridge University Press, 2024), pp. 587–8.

198 Margaret MacMillan, 'Making America Alone Again', *Foreign Affairs*, 21 July 2025, https://www.foreignaffairs.com/united-states/making-america-alone-again-alliances-margaret-macmillan.

199 Abraham Lincoln, 'Lyceum Address', 27 January 1838, Abraham Lincoln Online, https://www.abrahamlincolnonline.org/lincoln/speeches/lyceum.htm.

200 Michael Beckley, 'The Strange Triumph of a Broken America: Why Power Abroad Comes with Dysfunction at Home', *Foreign Affairs*, January/February 2025, https://www.foreignaffairs.com/united-states/strange-triumph-broken-america-michael-beckley.

201 Michael Beckley, 'The Age of American Unilateralism: How a Rogue Superpower Will Remake the Global Order', *Foreign Affairs*, 16 April 2025, https://www.foreignaffairs.com/united-states/age-american-unilateralism.

202 Logan Wright, 'China's Economy Has Peaked. Can Beijing Redefine Its Goals?', *China Leadership Monitor*, vol. 81, 1 September 2024, https://www.prcleader.org/post/china-s-economy-has-peaked-can-beijing-redefine-its-goals.

203 Emily Chen, 'Consumer Confidence Wanes as Investors Eye Opportunities in China', *Financial Analyst*, 14 January 2025, https://thefinancialanalyst.net/2025/01/14/consumer-confidence-wanes-as-investors-eye-opportunities-in-china/.

204 Derek Scissors, 'China Returns to Economic Maoism?', AEIdeas (American Enterprise Institute), 17 January 2025, https://www.aei.org/foreign-and-defense-policy/china-returns-to-economic-maoism/.

205 Yanzhong Huang, 'Tipped Power Balance: China's Peak and the U.S. Resilience', Council on Foreign Relations, 22 February 2024, https://www.cfr.org/blog/tipped-power-balance-chinas-peak-and-us-resilience.

206 Yan Xuetong, quoted in Orange Wang, 'China's Strength Gap with the US Will Widen as Competition Deepens, Top Political Scientist Says', *South China Morning Post*, 17 January 2024, https://www.scmp.com/news/china/diplomacy/article/3248647/chinas-strength-gap-us-will-widen-competition-deepens-top-political-scientist-says.

207 Nathan Beauchamp-Mustafaga and Howard Wang, 'The Threat from Overseas Chinese Military Bases Is Overblown', RAND, 1 August 2024, https://thediplomat.com/2024/07/the-threat-from-overseas-chinese-military-bases-is-overblown/.

208 Wang Yi, paraphrased in Nick Paton Walsh, 'China Tells EU It Can't Accept Russia Losing Its War Against Ukraine, Official Says', CNN, 4 July 2025, https://edition.cnn.com/2025/07/04/europe/china-ukraine-eu-war-intl.

209 András Rácz and Alina Hrytsenko, 'Partnership Short of Alliance: Military Cooperation Between Russia and China', Center for European Policy Analysis, 16 June 2025, https://cepa.org/comprehensive-reports/partnership-short-of-alliance-military-cooperation-between-russia-and-china/.

210 Huileng Tang, 'IMF Sees Russia's Wartime Economy Slowing After Two Strong Years', Business Insider, 30 July 2025, https://www.businessinsider.com/russia-economy-imf-downgrade-gdp-growth-outlook-wartime-boom-fast-2025-7.

211 Chris Donahue, quoted in Tim Zadorozhnyy, 'US General Says NATO Could Seize Russia's Kaliningrad with "Unheard of" Speed', *Kyiv Independent*, 18 July

2025, https://kyivindependent.com/us-general-says-nato-could-seize-russias-kaliningrad-unheard-of-fast/.

212 Jason Ma, 'Dow Futures Jump Nearly 400 Points as Markets Eye Another Serving of the TACO Trade After Trump Says "Don't Worry About China"', Fortune, 12 October 2025, https://fortune.com/2025/10/12/stock-market-today-dow-futures-trump-tariffs-china-trade-war-taco/.

213 Patricia Zengerle, 'Trump's Ukraine Plan Triggers Outrage from Republican Lawmakers', Reuters, 26 November 2025, https://www.reuters.com/world/us/trumps-ukraine-plan-triggers-outrage-republican-lawmakers-2025-11-26/.

214 Kori Schake, America vs the West: Can the Liberal World Order Survive? (Melbourne: Penguin Random House Australia, 2018), p. 8. Finnish President Alexander Stubb makes a similar argument for reconfiguring international order in the forthcoming January/February 2026 issue of Foreign Affairs.

215 'South Korea, China, Japan Agree to Promote Regional Trade as Trump Tariffs Loom', Reuters, 30 March 2025, https://www.reuters.com/world/asia-pacific/south-korea-china-japan-agree-promote-regional-trade-trump-tariffs-loom-2025-03-30/.

216 Fallows, 'How America Can Rise Again'.

217 Herman Wouk, The Caine Mutiny (New York: Back Bay Books, 1992 reprint).

218 Schake, The State and the Soldier, pp. 44–7.

219 Michael Beckley, 'The Age of American Unilateralism', Foreign Affairs, 16 April 2025, https://www.foreignaffairs.com/united-states/age-american-unilateralism.

220 'Debt Distress on China's BRI: Who Gets Bailed Out and Why?', Stanford Center on China's Economy and Institutions, https://sccei.fsi.stanford.edu/china-briefs/debt-distress-chinas-bri-who-gets-bailed-out-and-why.

221 Wolf, 'Trump's Assault on the Global Dollar'.

THE ADELPHI SERIES

Joshua Rovner

STRATEGY AND GRAND STRATEGY

Adelphi 514–515;
published January 2025;
234x156; 200pp;
Paperback: 978-1-041-02004-2
eBook: 978-1-003-61730-3

available at
amazon

OR

Routledge
Taylor & Francis Group

Adelphi 516;
published May 2025;
234x156; 156pp;
Paperback: 978-1-041-10132-1
eBook: 978-1-003-65351-6

Robert Ward

EVALUATING JAPAN'S NEW GRAND STRATEGY

IISS
THE INTERNATIONAL INSTITUTE
FOR STRATEGIC STUDIES

www.iiss.org/publications/adelphi

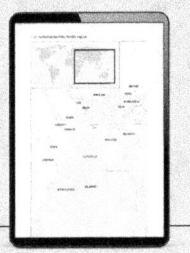

Six numbers of the *Adelphi* Series (Print ISSN 1944-5571, Online ISSN 1944-558X) are published each year by Taylor & Francis Group, 4 Park Square, Milton Park, Abingdon, Oxon, OX14 4RN, UK.

Send address changes to Taylor & Francis Customer Services, Informa UK Ltd., Sheepen Place, Colchester, Essex CO3 3LP, UK.

Subscription records are maintained at Taylor & Francis Group, 4 Park Square, Milton Park, Abingdon, OX14 4RN, UK.

Subscription information: For more information and subscription rates, please see tandfonline. com/pricing/journal/TADL). Taylor & Francis journals are available in a range of different packages, designed to suit every library's needs and budget. This journal is available for institutional subscriptions with online only or print & online options. This journal may also be available as part of our libraries, subject collections, or archives. For more information on our sales packages, please visit: librarianresources.taylorandfrancis.com.

For support with any institutional subscription, please visit help.tandfonline.com or email our dedicated team at subscriptions@tandf.co.uk.

Subscriptions purchased at the personal rate are strictly for personal, non-commercial use only. The reselling of personal subscriptions is prohibited. Personal subscriptions must be purchased with a personal check, credit card, or BAC/wire transfer. Proof of personal status may be requested.

Back issues: Please visit https://taylorandfrancis.com/journals/customer-services/ for more information on how to purchase back issues.

Ordering information: To subscribe to the Journal, please contact: T&F Customer Services, Informa UK Ltd, Sheepen Place, Colchester, Essex, CO3 3LP, United Kingdom. Tel: +44 (0) 20 8052 2030; email: subscriptions@tandf.co.uk.

Taylor & Francis journals are priced in USD, GBP and EUR (as well as AUD and CAD for a limited number of journals). All subscriptions are charged depending on where the end customer is based. If you are unsure which rate applies to you, please contact Customer Services. All subscriptions are payable in advance and all rates include postage. We are required to charge applicable VAT/ GST on all print and online combination subscriptions, in addition to our online only journals. Subscriptions are entered on an annual basis, i.e., January to December. Payment may be made by sterling cheque, dollar cheque, euro cheque, international money order, National Giro or credit card (Amex, Visa and Mastercard).

Permissions: See help.tandfonline.com/Librarian/s/article/Permissions.

Disclaimer: The International Institute for Strategic Studies and our publisher Informa UK Limited, trading as Taylor & Francis Group ("T&F"), make every effort to ensure the accuracy of all the information (the "Content") contained in our publications. However, the International Institute for Strategic Studies and our publisher T&F, our agents, and our licensors make no representations or warranties whatsoever as to the accuracy, completeness, or suitability for any purpose of the Content. Any opinions and views expressed in this publication are the opinions and views of the authors, and are not the views of or endorsed by the International Institute for Strategic Studies or our publisher T&F. The accuracy of the Content should not be relied upon and should be independently verified with primary sources of information and any reliance on the Content is at your own risk. The International Institute for Strategic Studies and our publisher T&F make no representations, warranties or guarantees, whether express or implied, that the Content is accurate, complete or up to date. The International Institute for Strategic Studies and our publisher T&F, shall not be liable for any losses, actions, claims, proceedings, demands, costs, expenses, damages, and other liabilities whatsoever or howsoever caused arising directly or indirectly in connection with, in relation to or arising out of the use of the Content. Full Terms & Conditions of access and use can be found at www.tandfonline.com/page/terms-and-conditions.

All Taylor & Francis Group journals are printed on paper from renewable sources by accredited partners.

For Product Safety Concerns and Information please contact our EU representative: GPSR@taylorandfrancis.com Taylor & Francis Verlag GmbH, Kaufingerstraße 24, 80331 München, Germany.

For Product Safety Concerns and Information please contact our EU
representative GPSR@taylorandfrancis.com
Taylor & Francis Verlag GmbH, Kaufingerstraße 24, 80331 München, Germany